CORN FLOWER

CORN FLOWER
CREATIVELY CANADIAN

WAYNE TOWNSEND

*to Mary —
Wayne Townsend*

NATURAL HERITAGE/NATURAL HISTORY INC

Corn Flower: Creatively Canadian
Wayne Townsend

Copyright © 2001 Wayne Townsend
All rights reserved. No portion of this book, with the exception of brief extracts for the purpose of literary or scholarly review, may be reproduced in any form without the permission of the publisher.

Published by Natural Heritage/Natural History Inc.
P.O. Box 95, Station O, Toronto, Ontario M4A 2M8

Canadian Cataloguing in Publication Data
Wayne Townsend
     Corn Flower: Creatively Canadian

Includes bibliographical references and index.
ISBN 1-896219-71-3

1. Hughes, W. J. (William John), 1881-1951. 2. W. J. Hughes and Sons Corn Flower Limited – History. 3. Cut glass – Canada – History. 4. Cut glass – Collectors and collecting – Canada. I. Title

NK5205.H83T68 2001   748.2911   C2001-930739-X

Cover and text design by Derek Chung Tiam Fook
Cover and all colour photography by Peter Herlihy
Edited by Jane Gibson
Printed and bound in Canada by Hignell Printing Limited, Winnipeg, Manitoba.

The Canada Council | Le Conseil des Arts
FOR THE ARTS | DU CANADA
SINCE 1957 | DEPUIS 1957

We acknowledge the financial support of the Government of Canada through the Book Publishing Industry Development Program (BPIDP) for our publishing activities, the support received for our publishing program from the Canada Council Block Grant Program and the assistance of the Association for the Export of Canadian Books, Ottawa.

Contents

Dedication   8

Acknowledgements   9

Introduction   11

Part One: The Dufferin Connection 1881–1912   15

Settlement in Dufferin County   18

Family Tragedy   26

From the Farm to the City   28

Marriage and Loss   32

Leadership in the Reorganized Church of Jesus Christ of Latter Day Saints   34

The Family Together at Wychwood   36

Part Two: Corn Flower and W. J. Hughes 1912–1951   39

A New Business Is Born   45

Early Corn Flower Pieces   49

A New Romance   53

The Business Expands   56

A Family Enterprise   59
Select Product Lines   61
On the Road   65
Jack Hughes, The Businessman   68
An Interest In Politics   76
The Family Man   78
During World War II   80
Renewal of Business   84
A Wedding In the Family   86
A New Partnership   88
Prosperous Times   90
The End of an Era   93

Colour Plates   97

Part Three: The Kayser Years 1951–1988   113
Hazel Hughes, Life Without Jack   116
Business in the Post War Years   118
The First Corn Flower Catalogue   125
Production Innovations and a New Plant   133
A Spectacular Showroom   136
New Cutting Frames, New Cutters   139
Moving the Business Forward   142
Retail Expansion   144
New Ideas   145
Changes for the Kaysers   148

Targeting the Bridal Market   149

New Marketing Strategies   154

New People, New Products   159

The Rise and Demise of Aluminum Trays   170

Premiums and Promotions   174

Open Stock and Quality Control   178

European Sources of Stemware   180

The 50th Anniversary   183

A Response to Increased Costs   185

Canadian Design is Recognized as Unique   190

Centennial Year and the Sixties   192

Another Kayser Joins the Company   196

A New Approach to Sales   199

Expanding Business in Hungary   201

Looking for New Lines   203

The Eighties   206

Epilogue: The Future of Corn Flower   211

Appendix I: Corn Flower Blanks: 1914-1944 (by Walter T. Lemiski)   216

Appendix II: Trademarks and "Copies" of Corn Flower   233

Appendix III: The Hughes Family Tree   235

Notes   243

Selected Bibliography   250

Credits for Visuals   251

Index   252

About the Author   256

Dedication

This book is dedicated to W. J. "Jack" Hughes of Dufferin County, for his creation, in 1912, of the Corn Flower cut glass pattern; to P.C. "Pete" Kayser for building Corn Flower into a major Canadian business; and to the Corn Flower Festival held annually at the Dufferin County Museum & Archives to honour Jack Hughes and his creative works.

Acknowledgements

I wish to acknowledge and thank the following people for their assistance in the development of this book on CORN FLOWER. Without them this could not have been produced; appreciation goes to:

Lois and Pete Kayser, Bobcaygeon, for their countless hours of time both recalling their stories and for the weeks of checking out facts and reviewing the chapters. Their friendship means much to me;

Krista Taylor, East Garafraxa, for her research, and for her involvement in the writing of chapter one. Her support of this book, of the Dufferin County Museum and of the CORN FLOWER collection is greatly appreciated;

Jan Crombie, Bailieboro, who urged Lois and Pete Kayser for many years to provide a reliable history and means of identification and recognition of CORN FLOWER glassware;

Barbara and Peter Sutton-Smith, Orillia, for bringing me together with Lois and Pete Kayser;

Walter and Kim Lemiski, Brampton, for their continued support of the Dufferin County Museum and for Walter's work on this book, and specifically his identification of the blanks;

Peter Herlihy, Orangeville, for his wonderful photography of the coloured CORN FLOWER used in this publication;

Jane Gibson and Barry Penhale, Natural Heritage, for their support of this project and for Jane's patience with my first attempt at writing;

Ken and Mildred Gamble, Shelburne, for telling me that CORN FLOWER was from Dufferin;

And our American friends who assisted with glass identification: Edward Goshe, Tiffin Glass Expert, and Emily Seate, Fostoria Glass Expert;

And the many others who supported and encouraged this project: George Pylypiuk, Alma and Orval Townsend, Steven J. Brown, Darrell Keenie, Karen Carruthers, Don Hughes, Mildred Taylor, Teressa Gray, Paul and Shirley Williamson, Hazel Gill, Lois Black, Susan Watt of the Archives of Ontario, and the Archives of the Reorganized Church of Jesus Christ of Latter Day Saints, Independence, Missouri.

While every effort has been made to authenticate the information in this book, the ultimate responsibility for accuracy is mine. There is always more to learn, and any information that readers can share with me is much appreciated.

Wayne Townsend
Orangeville, Ontario

Introduction

W. J. "Jack" Hughes (1881-1951), creator and manufacturer of CORN FLOWER. This portrait was used at the front of all company catalogues after Jack's death, until the company ceased operations.

For at least three generations of Canadians, CORN FLOWER cut glass products hold special memories. For some, it is a particular coloured cake plate that stood in Grandma's china cabinet. For another, it is the matched Candlewick tableware that came from guests on a wedding day more than 35 years ago. For some, it is an exceptional piece of CORN FLOWER found at an antique show that now sits proudly in the centre of a new owner's table.

CORN FLOWER is a pattern that is recognizable. It was produced and sold to Canadian working-class families who wished to add a bit of elegance and craftsmanship to their table, at a price that they could afford. It is interesting today that many CORN FLOWER collectors are the same type of people. They are both males and females who work at such jobs as teachers, truck drivers, retired politicians, nurses and farmers. For many, CORN FLOWER holds a special and personal memory of a family member or special event, the first piece in the collection. They all have the connection that brings history alive.

CORN FLOWER is a floral design cut in the surface of glassware by sandstone wheels. The design was created and developed by Dufferin County-born William John Hughes, known to everyone as Jack. The flower was cut with the hands of skilled Canadian craftsmen, onto blanks that were imported from various countries. As far as can be ascertained the design was never cut on Canadian-made glass.

The cutting of designs on glass had started centuries before W. J. Hughes was born. In the European country of Bohemia, craftsmen would remove the sand pebbles and flaws of their blown glass by cutting designs into the surface. Soon the shine and light refraction of the cuts was in demand in glassware, and the cuts were used to decorate areas where no imperfection existed. The term "cut" is used because the process involves taking away of material from the original stock or blank.

At the turn of the century the demand for good quality glass in Canada increased as the country became more affluent and moved out of the struggles of the pioneer period. Several companies such as Roden Brothers Silversmiths and Ellis-Ryrie of Toronto, along with Birks and Phillips Glass of Montreal, started cutting glass in Canada as an alternative to importing the finished product. Concentrating on lead crystal, a generation of craftsmen honed their skills. But, with the development of thinner, less expensive glass, people such as W. J. Hughes began to cut it with a lighter, less deep cut in new patterns on the new medium.

The cutting stones that remove the glass are surprisingly big and

Illustrations of the "five steps" used in the cutting of the CORN FLOWER design.

No. 1 'SPOTTING'
No. 2 'SIX-SIDING' (CENTRE) & 'STEMMING'
No. 3 'LEAFING'
No. 4 'PETALLING'
No. 5 'FRINGING' (TIPS OF PETALS)

cumbersome when compared to the fine, delicate cuts they create. Stones used to cut Corn Flower are about 5 to 8 inches in diameter and about 5/16 to 3/4 of an inch thick. The stones turn on a revolving spindle on the cutting frames, so the cutter must learn to hold and move each blank piece with the correct pressure for the right amount of time. Each cut is different and in a slightly different location on the blank so each piece is unique.

When W. J. Hughes designed the Corn Flower floral pattern, he made it in five different steps. The same five cuts were used on every piece of Corn Flower that left the company machines. First, the blank would be "spotted," marking the placement of the long lines that appear between the petals. The very first step for the cutter is to decide where and how many flowers would be cut on the piece of glass. Next, the steps known as "six-siding" and "stemming" add the diagonal cross-hatched flower centres and the stems coming from the centre. At Corn Flower these were cut with the same wheel. Thirdly, "leafing" adds the leaves to the stem, followed by the addition of the petals. The last process[7] called "fringing" or "nicking," adds the small hair lines to the ends of the petals.

It is impossible to tell the corporate history of Corn Flower without including family history as the two are so intertwined. This was an enterprise run in the family home with the family and the business sharing the same phone number. The family name was on the sticker of every piece of glass that they produced from 1932 to 1988. Indeed, the glass cutting factory and the family were only physically a staircase apart for W. J. Hughes and his wife and children. When Jack Hughes died, it was family, his daughter and son-in-law who continued the business. Their warm and vibrant personalities made them as memorable, for many, as the glass they cut and sold.

At a wedding reception in 1998 for a staff member of the Dufferin County Museum & Archives, a pitcher from the kitchen was used to serve water to the guests. Ken Gamble, who for many years had been the undertaker in Shelburne, commented to me that the pattern was called Corn Flower and that the man who had created it was from Dufferin County. As the curator of the museum which collects the material history of the people of Dufferin County, I thought how nice it would be if that were true. But I quickly corrected Ken and said that I had read that he was from England and had no connection to our community. He smiled and said that he would supply me with a family member who knew the true story, Don Hughes of Toronto.

Through the years much misinformation has been circulated about CORN FLOWER and the people who manufactured it. I hope that this book will correct those errors. From archival materials, by studying the collection of more than 450 pieces of CORN FLOWER that have been gathered at the Dufferin County Museum & Archives and from days of personal interviews and reviewing with the former operators of the company, Lois and Pete Kayser, I have attempted to tell the story of CORN FLOWER. This work is a tribute to its founder who left his own mark on Canadian manufacturing history. This is also a reference book for collectors both now and in the future. As pieces of CORN FLOWER are passed from one generation to the next, stories will be told of wedding gifts and birthday gifts, an amazing discovery at a yard sale and all sorts of special moments. Each story will be represented by a piece of glass cut with a combination of simple yet beautiful flowers and sprays of leaves. This pattern is known as CORN FLOWER, the story of which is told in *Corn Flower, Creatively Canadian*.

Wayne Townsend
Curator, Dufferin County Museum & Archives

PART ONE

The Dufferin Connections 1881-1912

IN APRIL 1881, DOMINION CENSUS TAKER THOMAS F. REID WAS travelling from farm to farm in the western part of Amaranth township, about 12 miles northwest of Orangeville, Ontario. Charged with the responsibility of asking questions on behalf of the federal government of John A. Macdonald, he was part of the second formal census taking of the young Dominion of Canada, a project intended to assess the population, age, origins and religious affiliations of all its inhabitants. For Reid, his job in the south end of the township was relatively easy. Here, established farms were laid out along well-made roads. But as he worked his way north and west, the roads dwindled and diminished into erratic blazed trails, and the farms took on the pioneer appearance of modest clearings in the dense woods.

The small hamlet of Bowling Green, located at the intersection of the Eighth Line and Ten Sideroad, was on the demarcation line between the settled and the later homesteading parts of the township. To the north and west lay partially cleared farm lots with primitive log buildings. Indeed many of these properties were still "bush lots," one hundred acres of trees which were farms only on paper and still waiting for the woodsman's axe. Although the rail line had gone through in 1872, much of the land was swampy and difficult to access, discouraging would-be settlers. The major impediment to actual settlement in the area, however, was the cluster of land speculators who held much of the property in anticipation of a greater return on their money. At that time, 100 acre lots in northwestern Amaranth were selling for $1800.

By 1881, Bowling Green supported a Methodist and an Anglican church, a general store, a one-room schoolhouse, a blacksmith shop, a post office and an Orange Lodge. Like most emerging hamlets of the later nineteenth century, Bowling Green had the necessities to take care of the body and the soul for the surrounding farming community. A good road led east to the village of Laurel, which boasted many of the same facilities, plus the all-important link — a railway station on the Toronto, Grey & Bruce Railway mainline from Toronto to Owen Sound, which in 1872 had made its way into Amaranth.

On April 18th, 1881, as Thomas Reid made his way west of Bowling Green by horse and buggy, he crossed over Willow Brook and then turned north on the Ninth Line. Before long, he came to the log house on the east half of lot 12, Concession 9, Amaranth. The farm was owned by Thomas Hinton, a neighbour, but rented to a family, Henry Hughes (1851–1937) and his wife Margaret Jane Armstrong (1857–1888), who had arrived in the township only four years earlier.

Thomas Reid recorded that Henry, aged 30, and Margaret, aged 24, were both born in Upper Canada and were of Irish origin. (The census did not ask, but the couple had originated in Lanark and Frontenac counties in eastern Ontario.) Thomas Reid documented the fact that Henry and Margaret had two children, Margaret Ann (Annie), aged 3, and Alfred, aged 1. Had Reid visited the Hughes five days later, he would have recorded two more names, twin boys. On April 22, 1881, William John (Jack) and Robert Edgar (Bob) Hughes were born. The birth was remarkable only in the fact that both babies survived the ordeal of being born in primitive conditions. Such was the inauspicious beginning for Jack Hughes who became the creator and manufacturer of cut glassware with a pattern which became widely known both nationally and internationally as W. J. Hughes "Corn Flower."

Henry Hughes and his wife Margaret Jane Armstrong, both raised in eastern Ontario, moved westward to the Dufferin County area in 1877.

Settlement in Dufferin County

THE YEAR 1881 WAS A SIGNIFICANT ONE IN DUFFERIN COUNTY. ON January 24 of that year, Dufferin was officially incorporated as the youngest county in the province of Ontario. Made up of parts of the old Wellington, Simcoe and Grey counties, the new county designated Orangeville as its county town. That year, Orangeville was thriving. The arrival of the Toronto, Grey & Bruce Railway in 1871 set the stage for an economic boom that enabled the growing centre to survive the "stock market crash of '73" which affected all of North America. That devastation was further aggravated by the financial collapse of the Canadian Pacific Railway which wiped out many Canadian businesses as well as investors. Closer to home, the weather of the early 1870s ruined many farmers in southern Ontario with a severe, burning drought.

In 1881, the year Jack Hughes was born, the county of Dufferin was created. A Court House and a Land Registry were erected in Orangeville to serve the new county. Today, both of these structures are designated as "Historical Buildings" under the Ontario Heritage Act.

The sense of local prosperity, however, was heightened when Orangeville became the northern terminus of the Credit Valley Railway running from Toronto via Streetsville and Brampton. Prior to the construction of the rail lines in the 1860s, town merchants had actually built gravel roads, encouraging more trade to come into the town. By 1876 the building boom was underway,

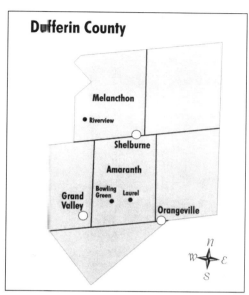

Map of Dufferin County

and nearly over by 1881, the year Orangeville was named County Town for the Dufferin. This significant designation meant an influx of professionals, mostly lawyers and bankers, and a heightened sense of prosperity. Many fine structures erected at that time still stand today. As an important trade and transportation hub, the town was able to support eleven hotels and three liquor stores, as well as a full range of grocery and other mercantile enterprises.

The new county now gave expression to the many changes in the region as the population of the area continued to increase steadily[1] and more land was cleared for farming. Most of the townships which made up the new county were no longer in the pioneer era of blazed trails and stump fields. The exceptions were Amaranth, Luther and Melancthon townships. Although located on some of the highest elevations in Ontario, much of the area is swampy and level; leftover melt water from the last glacial age is held in this section of Ontario. In the early 1880s, the section of Dufferin around Bowling Green, halfway across Amaranth, was still referred to as "the front," the edge of settled land. Closer to Orangeville, the area was well-established. To the north, Shelburne was beginning to develop into an aspiring town. In the cleared patches between settlements, brick and stone houses were appearing on family farms, replacing earlier log houses, and bank barns were in place of the old log stables.

Dufferin County, named for Frederick Temple Blackwood, Lord Dufferin,[2] had been settled predominately by Irish Protestants from the north of Ireland who had emigrated directly from the old country during the 1830s and early 1840s. Another significant influx of people came from the older settled areas further south, near Toronto, Brampton and Oakville, as the children of earlier emigrants moved northward during the late 1840s and early 1850s to find land, a commodity no longer available near their parents' farms.

This was the community into which the Hughes twins were born. Their arrival would have been of interest to their neighbours and relatives living in the district. Although Henry and Margaret Jane had arrived in

Amaranth in 1877, they had several family members living nearby in the township, some of whom had been there for more than 20 years. Back in 1866, fresh from Lanark County, Henry's older brother, William Hughes (1838–1911), had purchased a farm near the present hamlet of Laurel and may well have been an influence on Henry's decision to move to Dufferin.

Laurel, previously known as the English Settlement and later as Richardson's Corners, was built on what originally had been a tract of 100 acres deeded from the Crown to John Brown in 1847. Due to the remoteness of the location, and as the area was not cleared and very swampy, Brown sold the property to Robert Cathcart, who in turn sold to Joseph Dixon. In 1861, Dixon severed 20 acres at the northwest corner of the lot and sold to James Spence who, that same year, became the first postmaster of the hamlet. By 1863, the name of Laurel was established and the settlement was well underway with St. Matthew's Anglican Church locating near the centre of the village. Soon after a Methodist church, a general store, a smithy, a brickyard and a few houses followed. In the 1880s, a Presbyterian church and a cheese factory were added. Laurel quickly took on an established appearance as builders made use of the red brick manufactured in the middle of the village by Matthew Stickney Gray, the local Primitive Methodist minister.[3]

Main Street, Laurel, Ontario, circa 1910. During this period the store and post office were operated by John Anthony and Maude (Dobbin) Hughes. W.J. Hughes was their cousin.

A year after his arrival, William Hughes purchased a lot in Laurel, and that same year, 1867, he married Mary Ann Cooney, daughter of Anthony Cooney, who for some time now had been a farmer in the Laurel district. William soon became established as a builder and contractor with a sideline — building caskets for the village. As soon as he was old enough, his son William Herbert (Herb) joined his father in the construction business. Many of the local brick schools, churches and homes in the district were erected by them. William's younger son, John Anthony (Tone) Hughes, was postmaster at Laurel and operator of the Laurel cheese factory, which was run as a co-operative.

William Hughes, as well, had followed other relatives to Amaranth township. His aunt, Margaret Hughes, who had married John Hamilton, was one of the first in the Hughes family to venture away from Lanark County. The Hamiltons, along with their kin, the Buchanans, left eastern Ontario in the 1840s and were among the first settlers in central Amaranth township, then part of Wellington County. By 1853, Margaret and John Hamilton completed the purchase of their 200 acre farm near Laurel and were well-settled in the community. Amaranth township would not be incorporated until late 1854 and would elect its first council in January 1855.[4]

The Hughes family was of Irish origin with a strong attachment to the Church of England. Henry and William's father, John Hughes (1806–1902), was born in Ireland and sailed from Belfast, bound for Upper Canada in 1821 along with an uncle whose name is unknown. In Canada, John married Abigail White (1805–1899) also an immigrant from Ireland, the County of Armagh. Following their marriage, John and Abigail made Lanark County their home. John's obituary in 1902 indicated that he and Abigail had a family of eleven children, two daughters and nine sons, with Henry being the youngest. In the 1851 census for South Sherbrooke township, the infant Henry is listed with seven of his brothers. Henry's two sisters and one brother are unaccounted for and may have already left their parents' home on lots 16 and 17, Concession 10, South Sherbrooke township.

Wm Herbert "Herb" Hughes (1869-1948) was the eldest son of William Hughes and Mary Ann Cooney. A contractor by trade, in later life he entered local politics and became Reeve of the town of Shelburne from 1942 to 1945. Photo circa 1922.

SETTLEMENT IN DUFFERIN COUNTY 21

In 1877, Henry Hughes brought his wife, Margaret Jane Armstrong, to Amaranth as a bride. Margaret, who had been born in Upper Canada, was the daughter of John Y. Armstrong and Ann Atcheson. She married Henry Hughes on January 2, 1877 in Oso township, Frontenac County. On November 25, 1877, their first child, Margaret Ann, was born in Amaranth township. According to the township assessment roll, the young couple lived with Henry's parents, who had arrived in the area in 1877, and his brother Joseph, on a farm owned by Thomas Hinton. It was in this home, on lot 12, Concession 9, Amaranth, that their next four children, Alfred, Jack, Bob and Flossie, were born.

Around the same time that Henry and Margaret moved to Amaranth, his cousin John Hughes and his wife Isabella were living on a farm near the hamlet of Whittington, also in Amaranth. This farm had originally been purchased from Elijah Hamilton[5] in May 1875, by another relative named Joseph Hughes, of Bathurst township in Lanark County. In 1877, John Hughes bought this farm from Joseph and Elizabeth Hughes who were still living in Bathurst township and who, according to the records, would appear to be his parents. Although John and Isabella Hughes and their children appear on the 1881 Dominion Census, once John sold the farm to yet another cousin, Samuel Hamilton, there is no record of where they went to live. Further study of the Hughes family may indicate that several relatives ventured from Lanark and settled in Dufferin County before moving on to other destinations.

In 1884, Henry and Margaret Hughes and their five children moved closer to the village of Laurel, renting the east half of lot 9, Concession 6, Amaranth. In 1886, Joseph Hewitt Hughes, their youngest son, was born. The family remained on this farm for another two years then moved a little further north to another rented farm, this time in Melancthon township, still in Dufferin County. This rented property was in the community of Riverview, near the headwaters of the Grand River. Seemingly, there is no obvious reason for the move, but Henry's parents, John and Abigail, along with his brother Joseph, who was still a bachelor, also relocated there and were renting another home on the same farm. One family lived in the frame house recently erected on the farm and one family in the primitive log cabin built in a nearby hollow by the earliest

John Hughes (1806-1902) of Lanark County, grandfather of W.J. Hughes.

Henry and Margaret Jane Hughes shown with their children (l-r): Margaret Ann, William John (Jack) and twin Robert, Joseph (the baby). Seated in front are Alfred and Florence, circa 1887.

SETTLEMENT IN DUFFERIN COUNTY 23

settlers on the farm.

Riverview, similar to Bowling Green and Laurel, was a small service community with churches, a general store, a blacksmith and other basic supports needed in a fledgling community. However, the area was still quite forested, not even as widely settled or cleared as Amaranth had been. Although Melancthon had a population of 3,099 in 1891 as compared to 2,799 for Amaranth, it was a much larger township and some areas were barely accessible. Uncleared bush lots were still readily available but for some reason Henry did not purchase immediately.

Riverview, however, was different in that a new form of Christianity had found a home in the area. A congregation of the Reorganized Church of Jesus Christ of Latter Day Saints (RLDS) was established there in 1883 by a church appointee from the United States, J. A. McIntosh, with assistance from a local missionary. This local person was John Hamilton from Egremont township, part of Grey County, somewhat further west of Melancthon. Emerging during a time of great stress in rural areas in the mid 1880s to 1890s, this new church appeared to meet the needs of the residents of the Riverview district. A different form of worship was being provided to this rural congregation. The RLDS church challenged established churches, believing them to have become complacent in their ministry. With no formally trained priests or ministers, the new church presented beliefs that were open to individual interpretation.

By examining four of the beliefs it may be clear why the movement attracted the Protestant farmers in the area. The "Epitome of Faith" indicates that the church offered a less rigid style of worship, where layman were permitted to have their own modern day revelations. Secondly, the average farmer could become a member of the priesthood if "called" by God, similar to the practice of the Methodists. Thirdly, the church prided itself on being based on the word of the Bible. The only non-traditional aspect of the church in comparison with the established Protestant churches, was the use of the *Book of Mormon* which supported the possibility of modern-day revelation and prophecy. Lastly, the RLDS church believed in modern-day prophets, beginning with Joseph Smith (1803–1844), who during the 1830s, received a group of 138 revelations from God. The church was American in origin and believed that the Kingdom of God would be established in North America.[6.]

The impact of the severe economic depression of the mid 1880s, felt again ten years later, created a desperate need for a feeling of hope in this life here on earth. The RLDS church which encouraged a belief in modern day revelation and prophecy provided followers with a new-found faith.[7] As missionaries from Southern Ontario and the northern United States often visited in Toronto and London, it is possible that a person in the area would have had contact with someone in the church. A missionary would have been invited, thus setting the stage for the formation of an alternative form of worship. Many of the Hughes' new neighbours were part of this new, and in many cases, controversial denomination.

Family Tragedy

In June 1888, tragedy struck the Hughes family. The local paper, *The Shelburne Economist* printed the following from the Riverview correspondent in the June 21st issue: "Mrs. Hughes, who has been dangerously ill for some time, is not expected to recover. We hear that Mr. Hughes is also sick." Margaret died the day before the paper was printed, on June 20th. The following week, the Riverview correspondent relayed the sad news to the readers of *The Economist*:

> "We are sorry to have to record the death of Mrs. Hughes which took place on Wednesday evening last. Mrs. Hughes leaves behind her husband and six small children to mourn their loss. Mr. Hughes has the sympathy of the people of this vicinity in his sad bereavement."

Jack and his brothers and sisters, ages two to ten, laid their mother to rest in a plot in Shelburne Cemetery, with no stone to mark her grave. Years later, in the 1940s, a simple marble stone was erected by Jack to the memory of his mother, Margaret, his grandparents and his Uncle Joseph.

With six mouths to feed, Henry Hughes took the risk in 1889 and bought the 193 acre farm on lot 15 and 16, Concession 6 SW Melancthon from Susan Riky of Shelburne. This was the farm they had rented since having moved there in 1888. Henry kept the farm until 1896 when he sold it to Frederick Jarvis, a lawyer and private money lender from Toronto who had been one of Henry's mortgagors. The family continued to live on the farm,[8] renting from Jarvis who later resold half of the farm, lot 15 to Alfred Hughes in 1902. The other half, lot 16, changed hands from Jarvis to Harry A. Scace in 1902.

Surrounded by his grandparents and immediate family, Jack grew up with his brothers and sisters in Melancthon township from 1888 until at least 1896. By this time he was 15 years old. Henry did not remarry while his children were at home and, with the assistance of family and friends, raised his four sons and two daughters. Income from his mixed farming on the generally poor, wet soil was scarcely more than a pittance, but the children had all the love their father could give them. From testimonies of those who knew Jack in later years, the caring he had for his family evidently began with the love he received as a child while living on this farm. Their frame-house home stands to this day.

Living under difficult financial circumstances and working long hours with no money for modern equipment, Henry could not afford to send his children, especially his sons, to school for more than a few years, even though the school at Riverview was located only one road over. Although Jack received a very limited formal education, he was taught the values of hard work, family and helping others. These values he would carry forward into his adult life.

From the Farm to the City

T HE 1890s IN SOUTHERN ONTARIO WAS A DECADE OF TRANSITION and progress. Agriculture was changing with the introduction of new machinery, such as self-tying binders and threshing machines with blowers. In many instances these inventions replaced manpower. As a result, agriculture moved beyond subsistence farming since more cleared land meant farmers could produce higher yields and therefore profit from sales of produce in a good year. With these innovations came

The main street of Shelburne as it looked around 1900. This town was the closest shopping centre for Jack Hughes when he lived at Riverview as a young boy.

the change in the landscape with the construction of brick homes and improved farm buildings. But good farm land was also becoming scarce. The family farm was developing and land in southern Ontario was, correspondingly, becoming more expensive when it was available for purchase, sometimes going for as much as $2,500 for 100 acres.

As a result, thousands of young men and women from across rural Ontario were forced to find land or employment elsewhere. Many went to northern Ontario, western Canada or into the United States, while others caught the train and headed to the urban centres. So when Jack Hughes left his father's farm for Toronto, sometime in the late 1890s, he was no different than thousands of other farm children who preceded

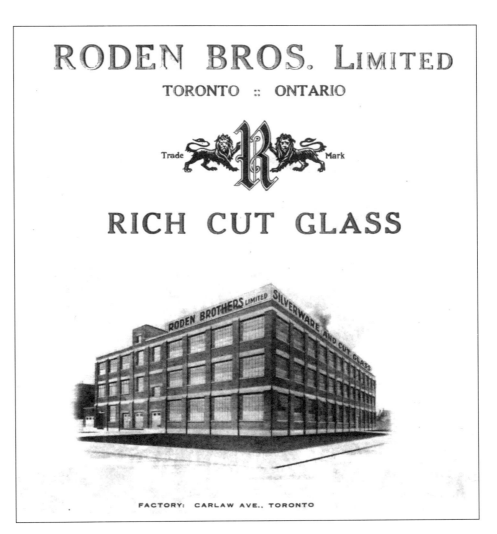

The Roden Brothers Limited logo and factory building as shown in a 1917 catalogue.

FROM THE FARM TO THE CITY 29

him or would follow in his steps. Like other young men, Jack sought employment by learning a trade as an apprentice.

The only known occupation that Jack had upon his arrival in the city were his various positions at Roden Brothers Silversmiths. However, it is not recorded as to how Jack made his way to this particular company. A young company, Roden Brothers Limited had established its operation in Toronto about 1891 and, by 1900, the business had moved to the Royal Opera House building at 245 Carlaw Avenue. Makers of sterling silver, they were also involved with a new process called silver-plating. At some point in 1907, they began cutting lead crystal glass.

Once established in Toronto, Jack was joined by his older sister, Annie, and her husband Melvin Hanna. This family had also originated in Lanark County and later relocated to Melancthon, where Melvin and Annie first lived after their marriage in June 1894 in Grand Valley, the service conducted by the Presbyterian minister, Reverend Hugh Crozier. Later that year, Annie joined the RLDS church at Riverview and Melvin joined a year later. By 1901, they had moved from Melvin's farm on lot 25, Concession 6 SW at Riverview, to Toronto. That same year, Jack Hughes was baptized into the Toronto RLDS Church.

Of the twin brothers, Robert was the quieter. After he, too, left Melancthon for Toronto, he worked at several different businesses before ultimately going to work for his brother Jack. The February 5, 1903 edition of *The Shelburne Free Press & Economist* gives us a glimpse of Robert's early adult life:

> "Robert Hughes and Rich Martin of Riverview, left Monday for North Bay, where they have engaged to work on the Ontario Government Railway now being constructed in the North Country."

Jack's other sister, Florence Beatrice (Flossie), married a local Dufferin County man, Isaac Stewart Ritchie, at her father's home near Riverview on December 24, 1902. They continued to live in Melancthon until they migrated west.

Robert Hughes, a formal photograph taken in Toronto circa 1900. Bob, the twin brother of W.J. (Jack) would have been about 20 years of age. This photo was made into a postcard.

FROM THE FARM TO THE CITY 31

Marriage and Loss

IN TORONTO IN 1903, JACK WAS MARRIED FOR THE FIRST TIME TO Martha Ann Hattey, daughter of Thomas and Elizabeth Mary Hattey. Born in 1881 on Manitoulin Island, she and her parents were involved with the RLDS church. It is most likely that the two young people met at a social event held there. The marriage ceremony which took place on November 4, was performed by A.E. Mortimer, a RLDS church elder. Both the bride and groom were recorded as being age 22 and residing in Toronto. Jack was listed as a jeweller and Martha as a spinster. Jack's sister Annie and brother-in-law Melvin were the witnesses to the marriage.

After his marriage, Jack continued working for Roden Brothers and lived in the St. Claren and Camden area east of the Don River in Toronto, not far from the Roden factory. However, less than one year later Jack lost both his wife and his infant daughter. Martha died September 10, 1904, of uremic convulsions. Seventeen days later their daughter, Bertha Evelyn, died. Both were buried in Mount Pleasant Cemetery in Toronto.

In 1904, Jack's father Henry moved close to his son in Toronto, leaving Alfred and his bride on the farm at Riverview. In 1902, Alfred had taken over the

W.J. Hughes and his first wife Martha Ann Hattey, circa 1903.

W.J. "Jack" Hughes at the grave of his first wife, Martha Hattey, in 190?, in Mount Pleasant Cemetery, Toronto.

renting of the farm from his father and had purchased it back from Frederick Jarvis. Two years later, in June of 1904, he had wed Phoebe McAdam of Beeton, Ontario.

In March 1908, Jack married again, this time to Annie Agatha Albina Swainson, a sister of his good friend from church, Earl Swainson. Annie, born in Lambton County on November 16, 1880, was the daughter of John G. Swainson (born in England in 1852) and Margaret Hayes (1855 - 1932). Little information surrounding the marriage of Jack and Annie has survived.

Leadership in the Reorganized Church of Jesus Christ of Latter Day Saints

IN 1905, JACK BUILT HIS NEW HOME AT 212 WYCHWOOD AVENUE, where Annie would join him following their wedding. He stayed with his work at Roden Brothers and became even more involved with the RLDS church. Beginning that year, he became the president of the church's auxiliary known as the "Religio," a group likely responsible for social and fundraising activities. Four years later, he was ordained to the priesthood office of teacher. The priesthood in the RLDS church is composed primarily of lay preachers, who become ministers through the calling of prophecy. Jack's calling of "teacher" indicates he possessed characteristics that would enable him to fulfill the duties of this calling. A teacher, part of the Aaronic Priesthood[9] in the church, is required to be a specialist in the field of human relations. The primary goal is to promote the ideal of being "good Christians." Hence, the duty of the teacher was to watch over the congregation and to strengthen it. Jack's life experiences to date included much heartache and, being accustomed to helping others, he would have been able to relate well and provide spiritual counselling.

In 1910, Jack was presented with a framed plaque and a chair from the auxiliary, upon being elected for a fifth term as the group's president. This plaque has been donated to the Dufferin County Museum by the Hughes family. The handwritten and illustrated message reads as follows:

"Dear Brother Hughes,
The members of the Religio desire to congratulate you in entering

upon your fifth term of office as its President. Since your first election to this position our Local has made unprecedented progress: our membership has been nearly doubled, our finances have become stronger, and in many ways the Society has fully vindicated its title of "Auxiliary to the Church."

Perhaps much of the seed that has borne fruit during your tenure of office was sown before your time. We may not apprehend clearly every cause of our success, but the results are apparent, and we speak of them with neither prejudice against your predecessors nor a desire to flatter you. Flattery is poor praise at best. Notes of thanks and material gifts are often gratifying, but the sweetest recompence (sic) of all is the consciousness that you have done your duty and always hewed to the line no matter where the chips might fall.

We have thought that a word of appreciation might serve to encourage you just now and so we speak it, and by way of substantiation that word we ask you to kindly accept this Morris Chair as betokening the esteem in which you are held by your fellow Religians.

Permit us in concluding to wish you and Sister Hughes continued Health and Happiness while we cherish the hope that our associations may reach through all our mortal years and renewed to "All Eternity" when we meet "beyond the River."

From the Toronto Local of Z. R. L. S. Jan. 21, 1910"

Evidently, Jack Hughes' talents for leadership and management were recognized prior to his becoming his own boss. He remained a member of the church until his death in 1951.

The Family Together at Wychwood

Jack Hughes and his second wife Annie Swainson, date unknown.

BY THE YEAR 1912, JACK, HIS FATHER HENRY AND BROTHER ALFRED had relocated to York township. On what would become Wychwood Avenue in the Bathurst Street/St. Clair Avenue area of Toronto, all three men had constructed their own homes. Jack's twin brother, Bob, and his wife, Minnie, lived directly behind Wychwood on Pinewood Avenue.

That year, his father Henry remarried, this time to Antoinette Gracey. They lived at 174 Wychwood, where he would remain until his death in 1937. After his move to his new home, Henry grew vegetables and purchased a push-cart to sell them in the neighbourhood. Alfred had sold the farm in Melancthon in 1906 and shortly afterwards came to Toronto with his wife Phoebe. He, too, was employed at Roden Brothers where he became a competent glass cutter, and later would build a home on the same street as his brother and his father. Records indicate that Alfred died at his home at 170 Wychwood Avenue in 1920; his death certificate indicates that he had lived there for nine years. However, it was Jack's home on 212 Wychwood Avenue that became an address that would long be associated with the future business of CORN FLOWER.

Jack's two sisters and youngest brother Joseph had moved out of Ontario. By 1914, Annie and Melvin had moved to Calgary and Flossie and Isaac Ritchie had relocated to Manitoba. Joseph, Jack's youngest brother, had also left his Dufferin home by 1901 and spent some time in California before returning to Toronto where he would die at Jack's residence in 1935.

From the humble beginnings of a poor farm boy in Dufferin County to a self-educated businessman in Toronto, Jack Hughes had achieved a great deal in a short time. Yet the lessons and experiences of his childhood never left him. He had been raised on the rugged edge of a county that was less than hospitable to farming, but close enough to both the rich, well-established farms and the prosperity of Orangeville to know that

A view of 212 Wychwood Avenue, Toronto circa 1920. Built circa 1910 by W.J. "Jack" Hughes, it would be his home until his death. By 1914, Jack Hughes was cutting CORN FLOWER in the basement of this building, his home.

THE FAMILY TOGETHER AT WYCHWOOD 37

there was a better life achieved by hard work and a bit of opportunity. Family and a diligent work ethic remained constant in his life. By the time he went into business for himself he owned his own home and was an esteemed member of his church. Although Jack had suffered the loss of his mother at the age of seven, the death of his first wife and child when he was only 23, and later the loss of another wife while in his early forties, he continued to strive for success and excellence in both his work and his life.

PART TWO

Corn Flower and W. J. Hughes 1912-1951

JACK HUGHES HAD LEARNED MUCH ABOUT THE CUTTING OF GLASS and the giftware business while working at Roden Brothers Limited, Silverware and Cut Glass. The company, owned by Frank and Thomas Roden, was a popular, successful silver firm, located on Carlaw Avenue in the east end of Toronto. Jack had started to work there around 1901 when he was about twenty years of age. Initially, he was assigned to what is referred to as the "metal room," where he measured and distributed the silver for the silvering process. Jack was not overly enthusiastic about the responsibility involved as silver was very expensive. One mistake would have cost much more than the wages he was earning. While on the job, Jack's outgoing personality won him friends in many of the various departments at the firm. He proved to be a very hard worker, eager to build a better life for himself.

When Roden Brothers began cutting lead crystal in 1907, Jack was offered an opportunity to learn the fine art of glass cutting. Within a few years, he had advanced to become "foreman of the cutting shop." Seemingly, W. J. Hughes had a natural gift for understanding how glass was made and shaped. By applying this intuitive sense to his skilful ability of cutting the glass so that it would catch the rays of light, Jack turned his lead crystal pieces into sparkling works of art. Roden Brothers catalogues of the period show that many of the firm's patterns were floral petals and leaves with such "cut" names as aster, mayflower, daisy, poppy, sunflower and cornflower.

As Jack often recalled to family members, his ambition was to go into business for himself. In 1912, he used his available funds to build a cutting frame for creating designs on glass and had it set up in the basement of his home on Wychwood Avenue. After purchasing some cutting wheels and, when not working at his job at the Rodens' firm, he started experimenting with cutting different patterns and designs of his own. His business began once he purchased one "barrel" of assorted glass blanks.[1] Working well into the evening hours, Jack would cut his designs on the blanks. Once he had sufficient product, he approached his retail friends whom he had met as a member of the Canadian Jewellers Association. Would any of his work have sufficient appeal to sell to their customers? Once a piece was sold, he would cut another as a replacement.

Jack decided that he preferred the more delicate "gray cutting"[2] on thinner "elegant" glass blanks to the "deep cutting" in thicker lead crystal that he helped to create at Roden Brothers. The fact that the prices of the "elegant" glass blanks, all of which were either mouth blown or handmade, were much more reasonable in cost than the heavy lead crystal being produced at the time also contributed to his preference. Jack cut a variety of patterns, but as floral designs were much in vogue, he particularly experimented with those he thought might be appealing to glass lovers. One of his personal favourites was a particular floral creation, a flower with twelve petals. The flower had an unusual centre, a hexagonal grid created by lines crossing each other in two directions. The distinctiveness was enhanced by flowing graceful stems and leaves around the flower.

Hughes also cut a geometrical pattern which he called "Royal." The Royal design featured a series of criss-cross lines at the lip of the stemware, with a line dropping from the centre of the cross, and was only ever cut on stemware.[3] From Jack's perspective, the Royal design took much longer to "cut" than the floral pattern because of the many repetitive cuts required. Once Jack started to hire and pay cutters, more

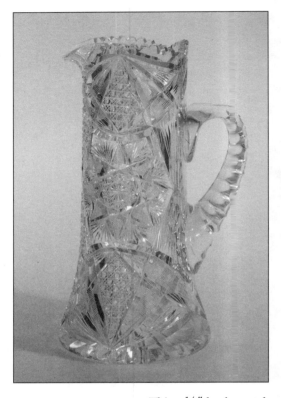

This 11½" lead crystal pitcher was cut circa 1910 by W.J. "Jack" Hughes while he was employed by Roden Brothers of Toronto. The pitcher is owned by his daughter, Lois Kayser.

Samples of deep cut, lead crystal products as shown in the Roden Brothers catalogue of 1917. Floral patterns, including a design called cornflower, were popular. Jack Hughes would have been involved in cutting these patterns.

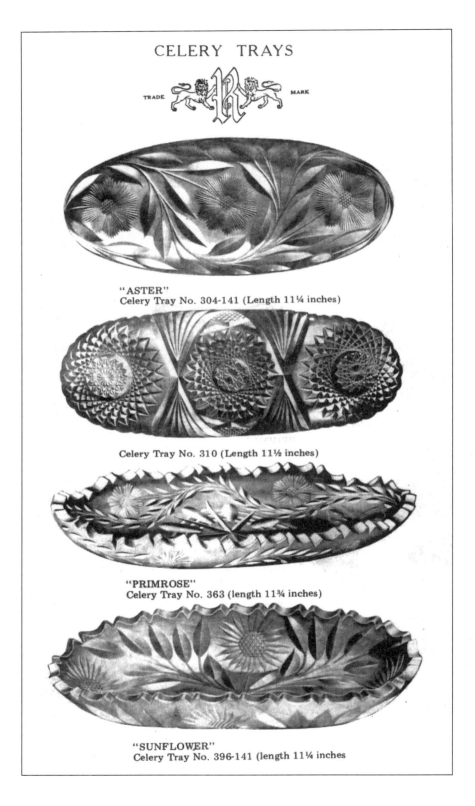

The catalogue pages show the details of design and of the skilled cuttings produced by the Roden firm.

CELERY TRAYS

"ASTER"
Celery Tray No. 304-141 (Length 11¼ inches)

Celery Tray No. 310 (Length 11½ inches)

"PRIMROSE"
Celery Tray No. 363 (length 11¾ inches)

"SUNFLOWER"
Celery Tray No. 396-141 (length 11¼ inches)

This dish, from a mouth blown blank, is an excellent example of the cut, known as beading, on the top edge of many of the early CORN FLOWER products that identify the piece as having perhaps been cut by W.J. Hughes himself in the 1920s.

Heisey Glass Company oval 9½" bowl.[4] The bowl has the embossed Heisey mark inside the bowl, circa 1917. In that period larger floral patterns (about 2½") with smaller centres and buds were used. The cut is deeper and shows the transition Jack Hughes made from deep cut to gray cut.

time also meant more costs, and less profit.

Many of W. J. Hughes' remarkable early experimental pieces may never be identified as his work, as these were neither labelled nor photographed. It is only in the memory of those who visited W. J. Hughes' early showroom and glass museum, set up in the basement of his home to display his special blanks and work, that it is known these cuts ever existed. Some pieces were cut with birds, moons, florals and geometric patterns as is evident from some of these pieces appearing in the background of family photos taken in the Hughes home at 212 Wychwood.

Catalogue photograph of the "Royal" stemware cut by W.J. Hughes in addition to his CORN FLOWER line, until at least 1940. This pattern took the cutters much longer to complete than did the CORN FLOWER design.

This picture frame was one of the other earlier cuts done by W.J. "Jack" Hughes that was not the familiar CORN FLOWER design. This frame shows his extraordinary abilities as a cutter.

44 CORN FLOWER - CREATIVELY CANADIAN

A New Business is Born

IN 1914, JACK TOLD THE RODEN FIRM THAT HE WAS GOING TO LEAVE the company to try his hand in the glass cutting business himself. By now his CORN FLOWER sales had grown to the point that Jack could no longer run the business as a part-time venture. He assured Mr. Roden that he would not be working as competition since Jack was planning to produce only gray cut glass products, a line that Roden Brothers did not offer. Working for the Roden firm would be the only full-time employee position Jack would ever hold. From that time on he was in business for himself.

Jack Hughes was a perfectionist. Only the absolutely flawless pieces made it to the retail stores, but mistakes were costly. From the very beginning, the pieces that Jack did not believe to be perfect, or what he thought to be "seconds," were sold to his friends or neighbours. Walter McKillop (now of Brampton) recalls boarding as a teenager along Wychwood and seeing Jack Hughes selling these "seconds" door-to-door in his neighbourhood.[5] Some of these folks did not have the means to afford cut glass at retail value. In the 1920s, a piece of cut stemware would have cost less than 25¢ for any item. The Eaton's catalogue of the time was selling a heavy lead, hand-cut line at $3.84 a dozen, a cost beyond the means of many. Jack had not forgotten what it was like to be poor and how a simple luxury item could bring joy to a family.

As he sold the glass he had cut, Jack would use the profits from his sales to purchase another wooden barrel of glass blanks, ordered through the glass salesmen and shipped from the United States by rail. No known

Canadian source of glass was used by W. J. Hughes as much of the glass produced in Ontario was of a much lesser quality and used mainly for such products as jars, window glass and bottles. Since fine quality glass required enormous heat, the limited amount of available natural gas or coal for use in Ontario may have been a contributing factor. By this time, most of the Canadian factories that produced "pressed" glass from 1870 to 1900 were closed.

Early in his business career, Jack learned that breakage could be very expensive. Jack told his family that "once he [Jack] fell off the steps of a streetcar while delivering an order to a Toronto retailer, dropping the box of cut glass and breaking the entire order."[6] Breakage incurred loss. From that time on, each piece was handled and packed with exceptional care, no matter how the order was being shipped or where delivered. The glass blanks arrived packed in "wool-wood," a substance called Excelsior, which was kept for future use. Composed of shredded, tangled bits of wood, this material was lighter than paper and absorbed the shocks of movement well. After being cut and washed, CORN FLOWER was repacked in the same material to be shipped to Jack's retail customers.

While the number of retail stores selling Jack Hughes' cut glass products in Toronto steadily increased, Jack's favourite customers were the owners of jewellery and gift stores in small southern Ontario towns. These places were familiar to him. The people were honest and loyal, with small town ideals. Many were involved with grassroots churches and lived "Christian" lives just like he did himself. These people reminded him of Dufferin County and his own roots and upbringing.

As he could not afford to maintain any inventory, Jack, within a few years of starting his business, decided to focus on his most popular design only, that being the floral cutting known as CORN FLOWER. Soon stemware, relish dishes, salt and pepper sets, cream and sugar sets, salad plates, bowls and many other items made by Hughes began to appear in retail stores in Toronto and across southern Ontario.

Starting a business during the years of World War One was difficult, if only because of the problem of acquiring even the small number of blanks he needed for cutting. In the United States many of the factories reduced production as the natural gas used to fuel their operations was needed for the war effort, or the glass being produced was used to manufacture essential supplies such as windshields and medical equipment. This, coupled with the absence of European glass, meant a more competitive market for those American glass blanks still being produced. Prices rose as decorating and gift shops, right across North America, were competing for the limited glass supplies. Jack had the advantage of being a one-man business. Fortunately, he could keep his expenses under control as there were no employees and, with his shop in the basement of his home, there was no rent to pay.

Little is known of his early years in business, but as the war finally drew to a close in 1918, Jack was cutting and selling Corn Flower to jewellery stores in Toronto and in smaller Ontario cities such as Guelph, Oshawa, Barrie and London, as well as to his already loyal customers in the small towns such as Orangeville, Shelburne, Alliston and Collingwood, among many others. Eaton's and Simpsons had become customers, although the exact years that they started carrying Corn Flower is not known. Both department stores had a loyal and steady clientele of middle-class Canadian working people, who seemed to like both the look and price of Corn Flower cut glass.

After WWI there was an increased prosperity and, as the boys returned home, many came to the arms of waiting sweethearts or returned with war brides. Weddings and parties were numerous, and gifts of stemware and tableware were popular selections. Today, many of the existing pieces of the early clear Corn Flower are family heirlooms that were originally gifts at Grandmother's wedding.

By the beginning of the 1920s, Jack was purchasing several barrels of fine quality glassware at a time. He consistently worked hard to pay the suppliers, as orders would not be shipped to him until the glass factory had been paid. With the postwar boom, it was critical to have sufficient blanks in stock. It was in this period that Jack, for the first time, began employing two or three glass cutters to increase production of Corn Flower items. Since glass cutting had been a popular trade from the 1890s right up to WWI, Jack was able to hire some experienced people, but he trained most of his employees himself. One was a young man named R.G. (Bobby) Sherriff[7] who started as an apprentice with Jack in 1923. He quickly learned the fine art and was soon recognized as an excellent cutter.

On May 20, 1923, Jack's second wife Annie died died of a stroke, at age 43. For twenty years she had suffered from mitral stenosis and had been seriously ill for the last year of her life. She is buried in the Mount Pleasant Mausoleum, built in 1920.

By the mid-1920s, the bright new colours of glass appearing in the marketplace quickly became popular items. Glass blanks were being produced in a variety of shades of green, yellow, amber, blue, pink, amethyst, and a small quantity of a yellow-green cast known as vaseline. During this period, blanks were purchased from top quality United States glass manufacturing companies, many of which were located in Ohio.[8]

Jack purchased his supplies from glass salesmen who had started to drop around at the small basement workshop. Some of these men represented several larger American glass factories, and Jack could browse through their catalogues and samples to find blanks that would suit not only CORN FLOWER cutting, but also the evolving tastes of the Ontario market. The Eaton's and Simpsons' catalogues of the period were beginning to sell more luxury items as well as their regular functional stock. With the rigid religious morals of the turn of the century becoming more relaxed, more and more items related to alcohol consumption, smoking and entertainment in the home were being promoted and purchased.

Jack made these glass salesmen feel welcome and often offered a meal with the family. Soon, the CORN FLOWER "factory" in the house on Wychwood Avenue became part of their regular round of business calls. From their catalogues, Jack purchased both clear and coloured glass of the period and cut the blanks with his increasingly popular and recognizable design. CORN FLOWER became known as a product of quality and affordable elegance with the expanding middle-class society of Ontario, the people who still comprised the largest market for Jack Hughes' products. For many of today's collectors, the coloured glass blanks of this period are the most sought after CORN FLOWER items, due to the beautiful combination of colour and cut.

Early Corn Flower Pieces

SEVERAL GLASS CUTTING DETAILS ON EARLY CLEAR AND COLOURED pieces cut from 1920 to 1940 help us to identify early CORN FLOWER pieces cut at the Hughes' shop. First is the design of the leaves in a horseshoe shape around the floral pattern. Many of Hughes' early work feature this pattern, usually in the centre of a plate or on a section of a divided piece. A second feature is the pattern of beading around the edges or bottom of the blank. "Beading" is a series of notches cut on a big wheel to make a type of pie-crust edge. This added to the overall distinctive look of the glass blank. Several different beading patterns have been found. The most common is a series of equally matched half ovals. A third detail is the CORN FLOWER "bud" which is a small bud shape used on cutting surfaces of the blank that were too small for a full flower. This bud has three small petals on the end of an oval cut and a stem. There is also a smaller "bud" version which was a small oval circle with three small lines coming from the top and a small straight stem. These have been found on candlesticks and narrow edges of plates and serving pieces. The underplates produced in this period often have the various buds. The fourth feature to watch for is a spray comprised of a small dot with a stem and three small leaves from each end. This has been found on a few very narrow edges. The next detail is a dot or notch added to handles to give a better grip and to add to the overall appearance. Lastly, sometimes several variations of a deep cut star appear on the bottom of various blanks.

A few of the early examples have other minor variations to these

Designs for some cuts used on early blanks (c.1914-1940) used by W.J. Hughes "Corn Flower": 1. spray 2. small bud 3. bud 4. beading or nicking 5. ovals on handles 6. bottom star.

added cuts, but the flower itself never changed. The number of petals used on the cut depended on the size of the cutting surface, but the standard number was twelve. An oversized flower can be found on the early pieces, but the design is consistent. In some pieces, available space was used by cutting large flowers, some between 2½ to 3 inches, with an abundance of leaves. On older pieces, as well, numerous flowers were used to fill the larger spaces on plates, bowls and compotes. The petals are always ground out of the glass with a cutting wheel, the surface of which is convex shaped and very smooth, and is referred to as a "flower stone."

Small hair lines coming from the end of the each petal are referred to as fringing or nicking. Nicking was cut, on early pieces, with a cutting wheel, shaped like an inverted "V," and with a very fine point. As each line

Clear stemware: 4½″ shell tumbler; 3½″ sherbet with underplate; 4″ tumbler and 6¼″ goblet. These were cut in the 1920s and display a much larger flower than pieces produced after 1940.

was cut individually, the spacing between each line would vary slightly. In the 1920s, one of Jack's cutters experimented with a wider cutting wheel with a slightly convex shaped surface, into which he cut adjacent grooves with a chisel-shaped diamond dressing tool, leaving fine ridges of the original surface between the grooves. This type of device, called a "gang-stone," meant he could cut several lines or nicks for the petal end, giving a uniform space between the fringes on the petal ends and decreasing the cutting time required for the fringing of the petals. By checking the space between fringes, collectors can date the earliest pieces by the non-uniform vs uniform nicking.

Coloured glass was used in a variety of ways in stemware. The complete item could be one colour, or the bowl of the item could be one colour with the stem and foot a different colour. Some stemware had a crystal (clear) bowl with a coloured stem and foot. Stemware items sold included goblets, sherbets, wines, cordials, footed water tumblers and footed juices, with the most popular items being goblets and sherbets.

In the early years, stemware blanks were purchased in small lots. As a result, consumers found it very difficult to match size, shape and colour, should an item be needed as a replacement or an addition to the number of a set. However, the 1920s were years of steady growth for CORN FLOWER.

The quantities of blanks ordered gradually increased until, in the late 1920s, stemware blanks were being purchased in "turn" lots,[9] which could number up to 600 pieces of an item, thus making it easier for consumers to match their stemware for replacement. As the selection and variety of tableware serving pieces increased, the demand for CORN FLOWER correspondingly increased. Across all of Ontario the design was becoming more recognized, and its popularity continued to spread by word of mouth. Marketing was helped by Jack's membership in the Canadian Jewellers' Association. With contacts in places right across Canada, he had clients in both the West and the Maritimes who would purchase from him when they came to Toronto.

At times there were problems. Some customers took too long to pay for shipments of CORN FLOWER. Sometimes glass factories were entangled in a range of production or union issues. Many of the American glass and ceramics factories were very involved with the labour movements of the 1920s, as were the railways that shipped the glass blanks. Thus, it was not always possible to rely on the prompt arrival of orders.

A close-up of the nicking of petals. Note the fine line coming from the end of the petal.

A New Romance

Hazel Graham, the newly graduated nurse.

Hazel Graham and the 1923 graduating nurses class of Grace Memorial Hospital in Toronto. Hazel is in the back row, second from the left.

I**N LATE 1923, JACK WAS SENT TO THE GRACE HOSPITAL IN TORONTO** for an appendectomy. By now he was 42 years old and twice a widower, but his life was about to change. In the hospital he lost not only his appendix but also his heart. Training in that facility was a young nurse named Hazel Graham. Born on September 3, 1900, on a small farm in Lutterworth township in the Haliburton area of Ontario, Hazel was one of six sisters and one brother. After finishing at her local school, Hazel attended and graduated from Grace Hospital School of Nursing in Toronto, part of the Graduating Class of 1923.

The city was a long way from home for the young girl, but she quickly made friends with her classmates and one in particular, named Jeanette Carr. They would remain friends over their entire lifespan. Since Jeanette was from Toronto, she was able to show her friend around the city. After Hazel graduated, she worked as a private nurse. One of her nursing assignments took her to Mono Mills in Dufferin County, not far from Jack's birthplace. How convenient it was for Jack to come back to Dufferin to visit relatives, and be able to pick up such an attractive girl on the way! It seems he would stop for Hazel at Mono Mills, then go on to visit his relatives in Dufferin virtually every Sunday. The folks at home had not seen so much of Jack in years. But they soon figured out the reason for his renewed interest and began to set out two extra plates. On each trip, gifts of CORN FLOWER glass were brought for assorted aunts and cousins. The fact that Hazel also had a sister, Florence Robinson, living on the Third Line of Albion township near Palgrave, not far from Jack's family in Dufferin, and another sister, Jesse McLeod, in Caledon only gave added incentive to visiting. Following a short courtship, the couple married on March 30, 1924.[10]

Two years later, in June 1926, their daughter Lois June was born. Always a very happy and active child, she was raised at 212 Wychwood, where all during her early years glassware stock, CORN FLOWER workers and the business operations were to be found in the basement of the family home. The Company and the family shared the phone, Melrose 8000, and Lois soon learned to answer the phone's ring with "W. J. Hughes." As a young girl, Lois was not interested in the business, but she loved to visit with her father's customers when they came to the house to purchase glass, although she was known to have kicked one or two in the shins if they teased her. One glass salesman, Jimmy Grogan, was a particular favourite, always bringing her candy when he came to sell.

It was evident that Lois' unending energy and sense of humour were a great addition to both the

Lois June Hughes, shown over the years, is the daughter of W.J. "Jack" Hughes and Hazel Graham. Top (l-r): Lois at age 2 in 1928; at age 5 in 1931. Bottom (l-r): Lois with her parents at age 11 in 1937; at age 17 in 1943. All of the photographs were taken at 212 Wychwood Avenue in Toronto.

The 1924 wedding certificate of W.J. "Jack" Hughes and Hazel Graham.

54   CORN FLOWER - CREATIVELY CANADIAN

home and the factory. As Lois became older, she did some cutting for fun and even typed some of the invoices. She remained involved with CORN FLOWER until the Company ceased production operations in 1988, a period spanning over 62 years.

The Business Expands

JACK CONTINUED TO DO ALL OF THE SELLING, PLUS SOME CUTTING, when at home. His employees, including his twin brother, Robert, came to work at Wychwood on a daily basis. Hazel Hughes washed, dried, inspected, labelled and wrapped every individual piece of glass that went through the cutting process in the small factory, now firmly established in their basement. Customers who intended to purchase glass for their stores and happened to arrive around the meal hour, were often asked to join the Hughes' family table. Suddenly an extra plate and food would appear from the kitchen. Over the weekend, friends from church frequently were dinner guests. For Hazel, there was much to be done for both family and the workshop. A quiet hard-working woman, she never drove a car and seemed to be satisfied being around her eight-room home, which she maintained above the "factory," as well as supporting her husband's work. Usually, it would be late at night before she finished.

During the twenties, Jack bought a new car and removed the back window from the vehicle. He took it to his cutting wheel and cut the CORN FLOWER design on the glass, then put the window back in place. Soon his car became readily recognized wherever he would go to sell his glassware. J. Sheldon "Shelly" Anderson, who worked as a watchmaker in J. Russell Morrow Jeweller in Orangeville from the late 1920s to the early 1930s, clearly remembered the car window when he was interviewed at the age of ninety.[11] Raised by practical Methodist farmers in Mono township, Shelly was amazed by this flashy and, from his perspective, useless adornment.

W.J. Hughes, the proud owner of a Model T Ford, circa 1918. Careful inspection of the back window shows the CORN FLOWER design.

The Hughes' home on Wychwood displayed many glass features cut by Jack. Hanging on the room panelling in the house were his mirrored glass reflectors, displaying scenes of water, skies with moons and stars, plants and birds. He would cut the patterns and then have them mirrored when he was having CORN FLOWER table reflectors silvered. Jack had added a product line of mirrors that were cut with CORN FLOWER, then coated with mirror-silvering at Toronto Glass & Mirror Company, which later became Advance Glass. There was also a line of mirrored glass picture frames, which came in both clear and blue, but were only in his product line for a short time. Instead of the CORN FLOWER design, they were cut with fruit patterns. Table reflector mirrors were not intended for hanging on walls, but rather to be put on all kinds of tables, under decorative objects or under table centrepieces to enhance their images in the reflective glass. Recently, reflective mirrors such as these had begun to appear in mail-order catalogues.

Some pressure was taken off the home when Jack's showroom for retail customers and his museum of glassware were moved next door to the basement of a duplex building he built at 214 Wychwood Avenue in

THE BUSINESS EXPANDS 57

the 1920s. Included in this museum and showroom were odd blanks with colours and shapes that he had fancied from the days of buying glass one or two dozen pieces at a time. He would often show this collection to customers and family members when they stopped in to buy or visit at the factory-home. That same year, immediately next door at 216 Wychwood, Jack also built a triplex which he rented out, but chose to maintain the building himself.

Many southern Ontario small towns had a day in the week when the shops would close, frequently a Wednesday. Retail store owners would then travel to Toronto by railway or car to purchase stock from wholesalers, CORN FLOWER always being a favourite. This practice allowed them to buy glassware items only as they needed them, and thereby save shipping charges as they would carry smaller orders back home themselves.

A Family Enterprise

MANY RELATIVES AND FRIENDS OF JACK HUGHES WERE EMPLOYED AT the CORN FLOWER factory. In this way he was able to assist his family financially and to surround himself with the people he most enjoyed. Raised without a mother, Jack remained close to his existing relatives throughout his lifetime, spending Sundays visiting and enjoying food with his or his wife's family members or church guests.

Jack Hughes surrounded himself with family. Pictured together in June 1928 are (l to r): Bob (Jack's twin), Jack and Hazel Hughes with daughter Lois (2 years old), Maude Hughes and "Tone" Hughes with their son Don, behind, Antoinette (Gracey) and Jack's father Henry. The building in the background is 214 Wychwood, where Jack relocated his showroom and museum in the 1920s.

Jack's twin brother, Bob (Robert Edgar) and his wife "Minnie" lived almost behind Jack at 77 Pinewood Avenue. They had two sons, Lloyd and Jack, and two daughters, Maizie and Hazel. During the early years the two families alternated Christmas and New Years in their homes. Bob, an entrepreneur like Jack, had tried his hand at a wholesale jewellery business and later, in the tire and battery business. As neither of these ventures were successful, he came to work for Jack as a glass cutter in the 1920s and, until his death, remained working with his twin brother. Bob's son, Lloyd, also worked for his Uncle Jack for many years.

Nearby, at 170 Wychwood, was Jack's brother Alfred and his wife Phoebe. Their sons, Cecil and Harold Hughes, were also employed by their Uncle Jack at various times. Almost next door to Alfred was their father, Henry who lived at 174 Wychwood Avenue. Lois remembers her grandfather giving her 25¢ "shinplasters" when she was a little girl. The youngest brother, Joseph, who had been in California for some time, became very ill with pernicious anemia and returned to Toronto to move in with Jack and Hazel. She provided nursing care for him in their home until Joseph died several months later.

In later years, Bill McAdam, who married Hazel Hughes' sister Annie, was employed to unwrap glass blanks and remove manufacturers' labels. George Scace, an old friend from back in Dufferin County, worked as a packer-shipper and prepared handwritten invoices. The Scace family had purchased the old Hughes' farm in Riverview some years earlier. Obviously, both family and friends played a significant role in the Hughes' enterprise.

When family members or guests from the church came to visit, Hazel would set her table with a unique grouping of tablepieces Jack had obtained for her. Her table setting consisted of salad plates, serving bowls, relish dishes, cream and sugar and candle holders, all in solid ruby glass, with sterling silver deposit decoration, not a CORN FLOWER product. At all times, however, the stemware was clear CORN FLOWER. Memories of these gatherings remain a part of the family stories passed down by the Hughes descendants. CORN FLOWER and the family would be the two focal points throughout the life of Jack Hughes.

Select Product Lines

Duringthe 1920s and 1930s clear stemware blanks were purchased in small lots, making it very difficult for consumers to match size, shape and colour, should an item be needed as a replacement or as an addition to a set. Conscious of this concern, Jack experimented with different shapes and styles of stemware, searching for the "right" shape to suit the customers who were buying Corn Flower. He ended his quest by selecting three different ones that had sold sufficiently well, requiring him to keep them consistently available to the consumers. These lines were designated by numbers: number 73, number 85 and number 196.

The number 73 line had straight sloping sides with a "stuck" tear-drop stem and was comprised of goblet, sherry, port, liqueur and footed juice glasses. The number 85 line had a concave or cup-shaped bowl with a tapered "drawn" stem and included goblet, sherbet, sherry, port, liqueur, footed water and footed juice. The 196 line had a tapered bowl with a slight flare at the rim and a slightly tapered "stuck" stem and included goblet, sherbet, tall sherbet or saucer champagne, wine cocktail, liqueur, footed water and footed juice. In later years, a larger cocktail, a larger wine and a flute champagne glass were added to the selection of items.

Only one invoice has survived from Corn Flower's early business years. On July 22, 1928, W. J. Hughes placed an order to Hammond, Turner & Sons Limited of Birmingham, England, "manufacturers of buttons, studs, links and electroplate smallware etc." for a full gross (144 pieces) of

Sample goblets showing the numbered lines of stemware that were selected to be consistently available to customers as open stock.

Number 73 – a bowl with straight sloping sides with a "stuck" tear-drop stem.

Number 85 – a cup-shaped bowl with a tapered "drawn" stem.

Number 196 – a tapered bowl with a slight flare at the rim and a slightly tapered "stuck" stem.

marmalade tops and spoons. The price of the tops was $2.16 per gross, and the spoons $3.00 per gross. Postage was $0.89, and insurance $0.06. That seemed like a large number of marmalade tops and spoons for a small glass cutting company operating out of a basement.

According to archival records, the CORN FLOWER foil labels were first used in 1932. Stanley Manufacturing of Toronto produced the labels eleven times, until the last order was made in 1941. There are no indications of quantities, but an order usually lasted about a year. The largest one was dated for August 1940, with the invoice indicating a cost of $66.00. The label soon established the identity of the CORN FLOWER product. This corporate trademark identifier would later play a role in distinguishing CORN FLOWER from the imitations that later began to appear.

CORN FLOWER products were sold through Eaton's mail-order catalogue, during a Christmas season in the 1930s.

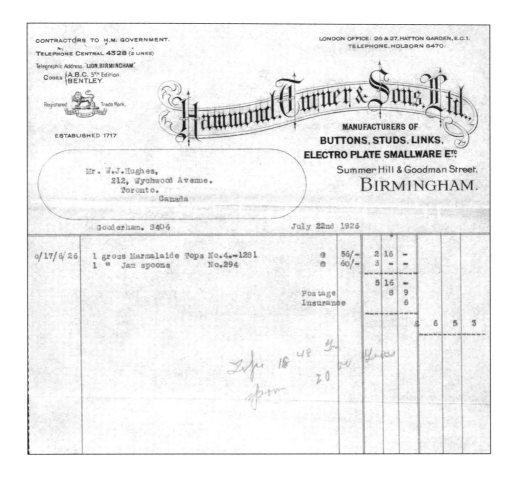

A challenge for collectors. This 1926 invoice indicates that somewhere there are marmalade pots cut with CORN FLOWER and with metal tops and spoons. No known examples exist to date.

The cover and a page from an early 1930s Eaton's gift Christmas Catalogue. CORN FLOWER was offered in all clear or with green or amber bases. This is the only known mail order catalogue to feature CORN FLOWER.

On the Road

As there were no hired sales persons, Jack would go on the road himself. It was his practice to visit his regular customers around southern Ontario at least twice a year, but as much as possible his selling runs were planned so that he would not be away from home overnight. On longer trips to Windsor or Ottawa, he would stay at hotels, but never be away any longer than absolutely necessary. Every trip would include visits to his retail customers such as Hogarth's of Napanee, Ontario, a business still very active today. Sometimes he would take his daughter Lois along. These were special outings for her, as normally Jack was very busy with business during the working week and could not spend much time with his family. Lois recalled her father commenting while they travelled, that the small stores in the little towns across Ontario were the most important customers to him. When they gave him a verbal order, it was a firm order, one which would not be cancelled. These people were the backbone of his business and very reliable as customers. He might receive an order from a department head in a large chain, but the store's principal buyer could cancel the order for something cheaper or from a more "favoured" supplier. As well, it was not uncommon for the large chains to ask for extended terms and discounts, whereas the "small" shopkeeper usually paid more promptly.

Selling trips anywhere near Dufferin County, where he would drop off stock at such stores as Morrow's Jewellers in Orangeville or George Watts Jewellery in Shelburne, would, without exception, include a quick visit with some of his many family members. The stop always meant a

CORN FLOWER gift to the lady of the house, or for any of her family who might be getting married and setting up house. Many of these gifts of stemware and tableware are still cherished by family descendants. Mildred Taylor of Grand Valley, daughter of Jean (Hughes) Young remembers Jack and Hazel visiting her grandparents, Henrietta "Jennie" and Herbert Hughes in Laurel during the 1930s. There would be gifts of Corn Flower, some of them "seconds." His relatives were also known to have taken orders from their friends, and these pieces would be delivered on the next trip through the area.

When Jack bought a new car, he always liked to pay cash for it. One of his joys was a large Nash touring car. In 1931, he took his wife Hazel and daughter Lois with him on a business trip, selling CORN FLOWER through the western provinces and on to British Columbia. With the hope of expanding business beyond Ontario, he, as a good businessman, visited existing customers along the way. Once the work portion was completed, he turned the trip into a holiday by extending their travels to California and back home through the United States. Ultimately, CORN FLOWER was selling across Canada, from the Maritimes to the west coast.

Jack Hughes always had a passion for the latest in automobiles. This photograph of a young Jack with his McLaughlin Touring Car is believed to have been taken at the side of the Roden Brothers factory circa 1926.

On one excursion into the western provinces in the mid 1930s, Jack was driving along a prairie road connecting the towns where he was making sales calls. The driver of a car behind him honked his horn several times. Jack, in his big Nash, was not about to have someone pass him on an open roadway. The faster Jack drove, the faster the car behind him drove, the horn blowing even more persistently the more rapidly they raced down the road. At a sudden turn Jack applied the brakes to slow down. Nothing happened. Jack and the Nash flew off the road, over a stone farm fence, across a field and stopped up against a barn. Amazingly there was little damage to his precious vehicle. The driver of the car, who had been following Jack so rigorously, ran up to see if he had been hurt. Upon seeing that Jack appeared uninjured, he explained, "I was blowing the horn to get you to stop. I wanted to tell you that your brake rod was hanging down below your car."[12] Later, Jack told his family that as he lay in bed that night in his hotel room, he heard sounds inside his head like water dripping into a tin pan. When he returned to Toronto, he found that he had a permanent heart ailment, assumed by the doctor to have been caused by the strain of the accident. He was never to take another long motor trip again.

As a result of his heart condition, Jack was unable to purchase life insurance, so he began to purchase real estate in Toronto and to build and rent duplexes in the neighbourhood to leave as equity for his family's future.

Jack Hughes, The Businessman

JACK HUGHES WAS KNOWN TO HAVE HAD CORN FLOWER CUT ON many odd blanks as special orders for his friends or customers. If the glass blank was manufactured in such a way that there was enough undecorated surface, it could be cut. CORN FLOWER, or another requested design would then be applied, often by Jack himself. Lois remembers "gift and jewellery store customers being offered this special cutting service as well. Dad would take the glass items away with him and return them on the next trip, cut as requested. The cost of the cutting was always kept to a minimum, as it was seen as good public relations, without costing very much money."[13] Glass cutters in the CORN FLOWER shop were also allowed to cut their own pieces on their own time, during lunch breaks and after work hours.

Although CORN FLOWER customers did not have much available cash for extra luxuries, the glassware made an excellent choice for a gift of quality, at a reasonable price. Throughout the 1930s, CORN FLOWER cut glass continued to grow in sales and popularity even though these were the Depression Years. For Jack and his business, the greatest difficulty of the Depression was getting his invoices for shipments to his customers paid in a reasonable time. However, he did appreciate that everyone was going through tough times, and indeed he went the "long mile" with many of his valued clients. Those who were able to pay, and did pay as promptly as possible, were greatly appreciated.

Jack had an interesting accounting system for the business. When a bill or invoice arrived, he would write a cheque and mail it the same day, maintaining his business reputation with his suppliers. He would then file the bill or invoice on top of the piano in the living room, where it would stay until the bookkeeper, Charles Waddell, came in, twice a year.

Jack's system of paying bills and invoices for glass blanks and other necessary items on the day he received them was greatly appreciated by the glass suppliers. The glass factory salesmen, convinced that Jack was a good credit risk, persuaded the factories to extend credit to Jack when he ordered blanks. His order would be made and shipped, with the invoice for payment following in the mail. These invoices were always paid promptly, and Jack always took the one percent discount offered for payment within 30 days of the date of the invoice.

Payment for glass shipments from American glass manufacturers could not be made directly from Jack to the manufacturers, as the American companies would not accept Canadian funds in payment for their merchandise. Jack would purchase a bank draft from his Canadian bank, in American funds drawn on a New York bank, in favour of the company he wished to pay. The amount would be equal to the invoice value, in United States funds. It is interesting to note that in the late forties the Canadian dollar was valued at 7% higher than its U.S. counterpart. Jack's bank would debit his account for the Canadian equivalent to the American dollar amount, plus a bank service fee and he would then mail the New York draft to the American supplier.

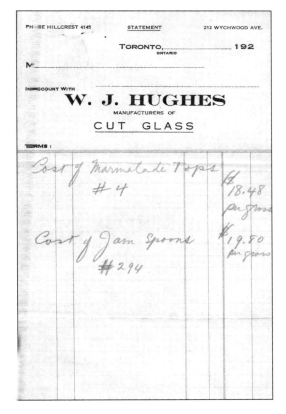

A note regarding a 1926 shipment in the handwriting of W.J. Hughes. While the early letterhead does show the address, it does not use the word CORN FLOWER.

Business continued to grow in the mid-to-late 1930s, and Jack reordered larger and larger quantities of glass blanks for cutting. As his orders increased, his credit rating in the glass industry became higher and higher. At the time of his death in 1951, there was no known limit to his credit.

Around 1937 Jack produced a type of "catalogue" in a series of photographs mounted on linen-backed paper showing some of his CORN FLOWER products. The photographs had been taken by J. Thornley Wrench, a commercial photographer operating from 225 Jarvis Street, Toronto. On the backs of the photographs, Jack had noted stock numbers, colours available listing rose, green, amber and yellow, and prices of the items. Most items were available in crystal (clear). These photographs still exist, and in 1999 were donated to the Dufferin County Museum & Archives. No full catalogue was produced until the early 1950s after Jack's death.

In the early days Jack had not employed salesmen to sell CORN FLOWER. The selling he had done himself, believing that the personal contact with his customers was of primary importance. However, in 1940, he entered into an agreement with a Toronto company, which had salesmen on the road, representing several different lines of giftware and jewellery. The company, Haddy, Body and Company of Toronto, covered all of Ontario. Jack provided the salesmen with his "catalogue" of photographs. Haddy, Body and Company were paid a commission on orders taken. Jack now had sufficient inventory of CORN FLOWER that he could deliver orders from stock. The days of a few barrels or odd lots of glass were well in the past.

Shortly before Canada entered WWII, Jack employed a young man named Mike Gray to learn the glass cutting trade. Mike was from a farm near Riverview in Dufferin County. He liked cutting glass and enjoyed the "clean" feel of the product with which he was working. According to his widow Theresa, Mike was personally rewarded with particular satisfaction when his delicate cutting produced a well-turned out item of cut glass.

With a more established salesforce in place, his photograph "catalogue" exposure and reliable cutters as employees, Jack Hughes was assured a bright future for his CORN FLOWER.

The wholesale price list of stemware as shown on company letterhead, circa late 1930s. Two particular shapes #196 and #73 are noted. The list is in W.J. Hughes' handwriting.

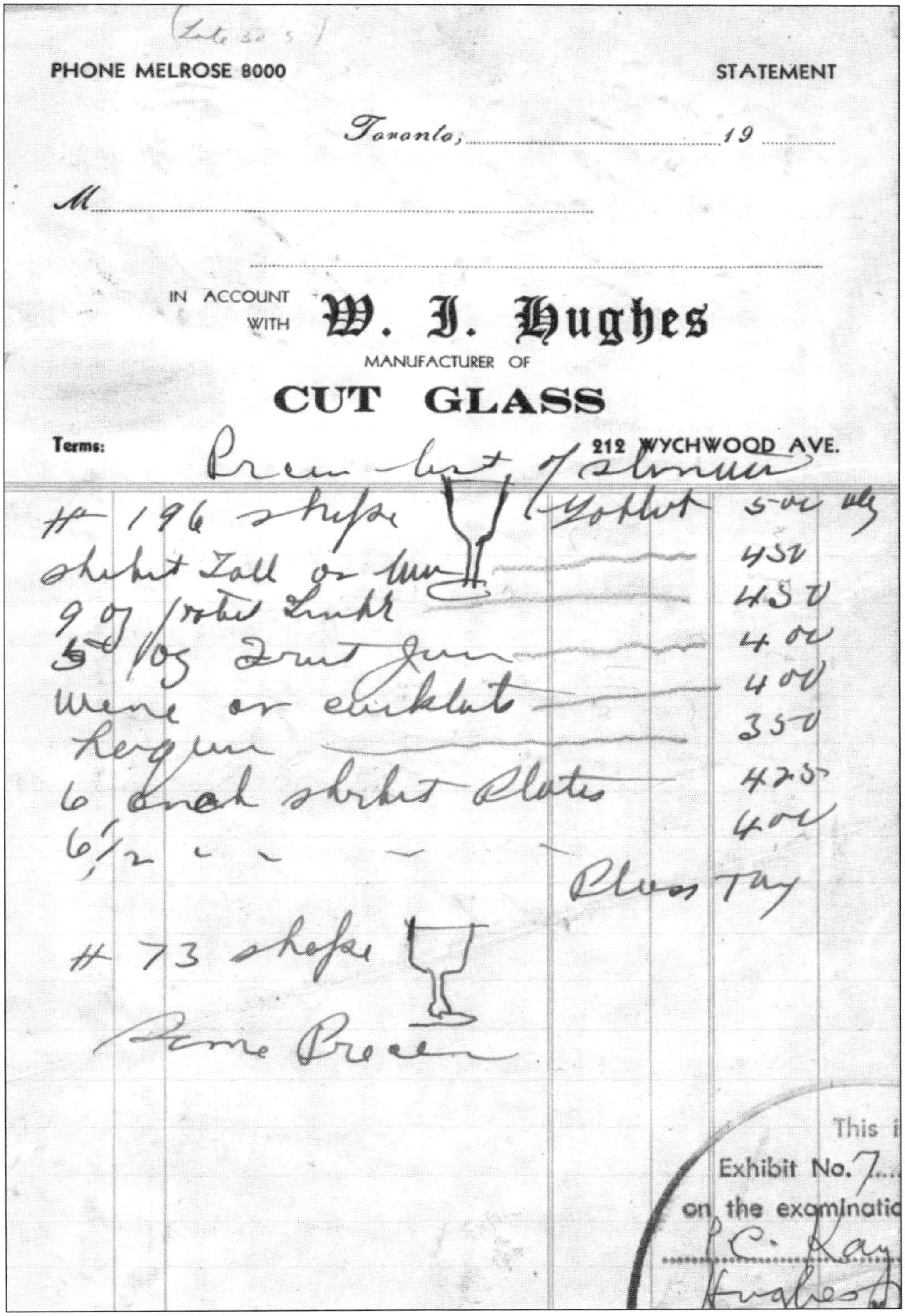

PHONE MELROSE 8000   STATEMENT

Toronto, _____ 19_____

M _____

IN ACCOUNT WITH **W. J. Hughes**
MANUFACTURER OF
CUT GLASS

Terms: 212 WYCHWOOD AVE.

[handwritten list, partially illegible]

Price list of stemware

#196 shape — Goblet   5 oz   4.50
Sherbet Tall or low   4.50
9 oz water tumbler   4.00
5/10 oz fruit juice   4.00
Wine or cocktail   3.50
Liqueur   4.25
6 inch sherbet plates   4.00
6½ " " "
       Cheese Tray

#73 shape

Same Price

Exhibit No. 7
on the examination

Photographs taken by J. Thornley Wrench for W.J. Hughes' first "catalogue," circa 1937.

top row:
3 Tiffin footed Table Tumblers #020
2 unattributed flat Tumblers

bottom row:
series of crystal Stems with amber and green trim (stems)

Series of unattributed 3-footed Bonbons

top row:
New Martinsville
No.412 crystal
Candy Box 3-
compartments;
1100 8" crystal Bowl;
No.412 1125 crystal
Candy Box

top row:
Attributed to Heisey
Ice/Butter Tub;
covered Marmalade
Jar;
footed Toothpick
Holder;
covered Butter Dish

bottom row:
#5831 Candelabrum;
2-litre 3-footed Bowl

Attributed to New Martinsville
top row: Muffin Tray; Sandwich Plate; handled 2-part Relish

bottom row: centre-handled Sandwich Tray; Flower Bowl with Frog

top row: Lemon Tray; Salad Plate; Sherbet Plate

bottom row: #176 Tumbler and Jug; #173 Tumbler and Jug

top row:
Whipped Cream;
oval Platter; Tiffin
#342 4" Candleholder

bottom row:
Syrup; Series of 4
Bud Vases;
Candlestick

top row:
Assorted items
attributed to Heisey
Glass Company

bottom row:
Flower Bowls with
Frogs

An Interest In Politics

From an early age Jack had an interest in politics. One of his contemporaries in both politics and church was Agnes Campbell Macphail. Born in Proton township, Grey County (not far from Riverview), in 1890, Agnes was a member of the RLDS church, and later a Member of Parliament, at both the federal and provincial levels, and was the first woman to be elected to the House of Commons. Macphail acquired a seat for the provincial riding of York East in the election of 1943 as a CCF candidate. Although defeated in 1945, she was returned as an MLA three years later. Jack's daughter Lois remembers Agnes Macphail visiting her parents at 212 Wychwood Ave. There were probably many lively discussions about both religion and politics when the three of them were together.

In the October 6, 1937 provincial election, William J. Hughes ran for MPP in York South, as an Independent Conservative. Although he only received 1% of the vote, that did not end his political involvement. Lois remembers that her father became involved with the Co-operative Commonwealth Federation (CCF) following his defeat in the 1937 election. The movement was composed of members who believed that the problems of the day, primarily the national Depression, could be solved by making changes in the economic social order. The roots of the CCF began with the Social Gospel movement and gradually became involved with the League for Social Reconstruction. Supporters believed human need was far more important than private profit and the only way to achieve change was through an organized and effective political

A W. J. Hughes "Cornflower" company cheque dated 1950 and signed by owner, W. J. Hughes. The cheque, made out to the C.C.F. News, indicates Jack's support of the political party.

structure.[14] One of several political groups growing out of the Great Depression and drought on the Prairies, the CCF hoped to bring together labour, farmer and political movements that otherwise had previously had no mutual interest in political or social change.

Jack's keen interest in the CCF may be explained by the attention given by the *Regina Manifesto* to the social concerns of the time. The *Regina Manifesto*, written for and presented at the first CCF meeting in 1933, called for a new social order with the elimination of domination and exploitation by one class over another. The written manifest took a stand on social planning, the national labour code, publicly organized health, trade, external affairs and taxation, among several other issues sensitive to the era and to Jack both personally and professionally.

With the continuation of the Depression, Jack as an entrepreneur was affected by the trade policies and taxation; it is not surprising that he became involved in politics.

The Family Man

Jack and Hazel had two more children. A son, Robert John, was born on June 6, 1939. The company name was then changed to "W. J. Hughes and Son." On August 13, 1940, just over a year later, another son Graham Harrison was born and the company was renamed "W. J. Hughes and Sons." The changes were added to the company letterhead, shipping labels and invoices, but the Corn Flower labels applied to the glassware never changed. With the arrival of the two boys, a helper was employed for washing, inspecting, applying labels and wrapping the glass in newspaper. Now Hazel was able to devote her time to raising the children. For sixteen years she had handled every piece of glass that had passed through their doors.

Throughout the Depression, Jack always wore a top quality diamond stickpin in his tie, and an equally significant diamond in a ring on each hand. First and foremost, he dealt with jewellers who knew quality, He always stated that "if a man is poor, there is no need to look poor."[15]

Despite this small show of wealth, Jack always remembered his humble beginnings, and was known far beyond Toronto for his generosity to the poor and unfortunate, especially those with small children. Throughout his entire adult life, he gave generously to charities, both in Toronto and back in Dufferin County.[16] He would also get names of the neediest families from the police in York township and deliver turkeys, toys and clothing to their homes for Christmas. This practice continued until his death.

Jack's hair was always neatly trimmed, and his shirts crisp and white.

A "bad" habit was the occasional cigar which his daughter Lois remembers as "cheap and smelly," especially when experienced in the car. Always handsome as a young man, he now liked to look the part of a smart successful businessman. His pretty wife and small children were the family that Jack had never had and his life was full of achievements that at one time he had only dared to dream about.

From Monday through Saturday Jack wore a dustcoat over his shirt and tie. When cutting glass, when going to the bank and when eating meals, whether in the heat of summer or the chill of winter, this protective layer was always in place. On summer Sundays he would wear a Palm Beach suit, carry a cane and sport a fine straw hat. Sundays were hard on Jack. His religious beliefs would not permit his working, but the sabbath days were harder on his family, since Jack simply did not know how to "do nothing," often taking to walking the floor and making family members uncomfortable. Sometimes he would take Sunday drives with his family, sometimes going to Palgrave to visit Hazel's widowed sister and her children. If he did stay at home, he would spend much of the time reading the Bible. But no matter what he did, his mind was always on the factory in the basement.

During World War II

JACK DID NOT ADVERTISE CORN FLOWER. HE DEVOTED HIS EFFORTS to providing a quality product and supplying a popular cut glass line with as many items as any discerning hostess could wish to put on her table or in her home. His search was unending and, when he added the Imperial Glass Corporation's "Candlewick" glass line in 1939, the results excelled anything in the past. That year he placed his first order for Candlewick blanks with Ed Kleiner, Imperial's Canadian representative based in New York City. Less than a year later, a verbal agreement was made between Jack Hughes and the American company, granting exclusive cutting rights of Imperial Glass Candlewick in Canada to W. J. Hughes and Sons. This agreement proved to be of great benefit to both companies. Imperial Candlewick cut with CORN FLOWER became the largest selling line of tableware items ever enhanced with CORN FLOWER.[17]

Imperial Candlewick is among the best known patterns ever made by an American glass manufacturer. Introduced circa 1936 as No. 400 Candlewick, it allowed Imperial Glass to survive during the 1930s and over 250 different Candlewick blanks were offered during the 1940s.[18]

Imperial Candlewick is easily recognized by the series of small "balls" that are used around the edges, on handles and other areas as decorative detail. W. J. Hughes "Corn Flower" used mostly the crystal (clear) Candlewick blanks, but three examples are known of an amber, 4-toed bowl made circa late 1930s. One is in the Dufferin County Museum Archives' collection; another was cut by Mike Gray as a gift to his wife Theresa and was broken; the third belongs to a descendant of Robert

Hughes, Jack's uncle. While some of Imperial's Pie Crust crystal No. 588 was used from the 1930s to the 1950s, it however, was never the popular seller that Candlewick became.

During the first years of World War II, Jack was unable to purchase a sufficient number of blanks for cutting to meet the orders he was receiving. In 1940, the Canadian government had imposed a quota on the amount of United States dollars that could be available to W. J. Hughes and Sons for the purchase of glass blanks for cutting. The government classified cut glass as a luxury and non-essential item during the war effort. A quota was established at 42% of the annual United States dollars spent by W. J. Hughes and Sons for imported blanks, averaged between the years 1938 and 1939.[19] These were the very years that business was booming for Jack. To be cut back to 42% was a serious set back for business in the following years, as glass blanks of the equivalent quality were not manufactured in Canada.

Most of the American glass factories used natural gas to fuel their glass furnaces. When natural gas was rationed to them once the United States entered the war in 1941, some of the factories converted a few of their furnaces to operate with oil as well as gas. Oil was more readily available, but much more expensive. As a result, production of glass was restricted, but the factories could keep the glass batches in the operating

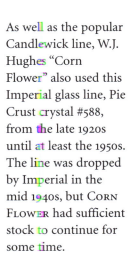

As well as the popular Candlewick line, W.J. Hughes "Corn Flower" also used this Imperial glass line, Pie Crust crystal #588, from the late 1920s until at least the 1950s. The line was dropped by Imperial in the mid 1940s, but CORN FLOWER had sufficient stock to continue for some time.

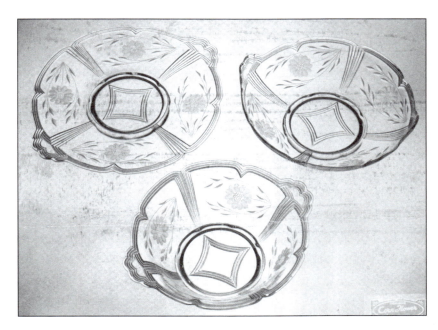

furnaces in a molten state. If a furnace had to be shut down, it would have to be rebuilt with new firebrick before production could be restarted. The start-up could take weeks by the time the new firebrick was installed in the furnace and "cured" and the new glass batch was "cleared," the point at which all the impurities from the new bricks are burned out and clear molten liquid is ready for production. As well, the younger glass workers and apprentices became scarce in American factories as employees enlisted or were drafted. Glassware was in short supply in the United States for the domestic market, but it was in even shorter supply for export to Canada. A search through archival papers found an invoice from the Ludwik Glass Company of Weston, West Virginia identifying an order dated October 24, 1943.[20] The order was for 762 dozen stemware blanks, with a cost price in U.S. dollars of $2.60 to $2.80 per dozen. It took almost 44 months for delivery.

William Morris "Mike" Gray (1923-1977). Mike was raised in Melancthan township as was W.J. Hughes a generation before. Mike cut CORN FLOWER both before and after he was in the RCAF during WWII.

In Europe, the major glass factories were in countries occupied by the Nazi forces. If any glassware had been made at the time, it would not have been exported to Canada. As well, during the war years many commodities were under government control. Prices of rents, goods, wages and a multitude of things were "frozen" by the government. The top glass cutter's wage at CORN FLOWER was frozen at $35.00 a week.

One of the glass cutters at the CORN FLOWER factory, Mike Gray, had enlisted in the air force and another, Lloyd Hughes, had been drafted into the army. "Bill" Curtis, who had started in the 1930s, and Bob Hughes continued cutting glass as by this time both were over the age limit for service. George Scace unwrapped, packed and shipped glass, and continued to write invoices by hand. Later, Mike's sister, Georgina Gray married Bud Peace, another cutter, strengthening the sense of family and friends at the CORN FLOWER factory.

Although many people left the Company to support the war effort, one person left for a totally different reason. Bobby Sherriff resigned from the company in 1940 to go into business for himself. He started by cutting a design he called "Cosmos." Shortly after leaving, he began to cut a copy of CORN FLOWER, a design well-known to him, having cut it for seventeen years. He went so far as to apply a label to the glass, featuring the same shape and colouring as the registered CORN FLOWER label. In 1948, Jack

This clear lemonade set has one tumbler with a paper W.J. Hughes 'Corn Flower' label. Paper labels were used instead of foil during WWII. Foil labels returned at the conclusion of the war, circa 1946.

commenced legal proceedings against R. G. Sherriff, with the result that the court ordered Sherriff to cease the use of the label or any similar label.

During the war, all families at home were encouraged, through a government campaign, to save foil from cigarette packages, candy wrap and anything that contained foil. These foil scraps were rolled into balls and turned in at depots set up for the war effort and recycled for re-use of the aluminum. Not surprisingly, foil was not available for the CORN FLOWER labels, hence gold-coloured paper with blue ink printing was used as a replacement. Unfortunately, the paper CORN FLOWER labels came off after the first few washings. To date, very few examples of these wartime labels are known to exist. One example is found on a tumbler of a clear 1940s lemonade set in the collection of CORN FLOWER at the Dufferin County Museum & Archives.

In the mid-to-late 1940s, Jack purchased two European-made items of interest to many collectors. These were a ruby-footed pilsner glass and a ruby-handled beer stein. It is not know for certain whether he purchased these items from Czechoslovakia or Poland and, seemingly, it took years for these to be shipped. But it is known that in 1949 the representative of the Polish glass factories contacted Jack and told him that another order for ruby-footed pilsner glasses was ready for shipment. These were shipped, cut and sold very quickly. The scarcity of these items, made more popular by their exceptional blood-red colour, makes them prized pieces in any collection. Subsequent orders for these glasses were never confirmed nor received.

Renewal of Business

I T IS KNOWN FROM SURVIVING ARCHIVAL MATERIALS, CHEQUES AND invoices, that from 1939 through the post war years until 1951, Jack purchased glass blanks from a variety of glass factories.[21] Before the war he had been buying stemware blanks from a factory in Czechoslovakia. In 1947, their agent based in New York City, advised Jack that glass production was once again available for shipment to Canada. Jack placed orders for the three shapes of stemware that had become his regular stock lines before the war, the shapes identified as #73, #85 and #196. The #73 and #85 lines had been least available during the war years, as he had only received some with similar shapes from American sources during the war. Hence, Jack asked that these be made and shipped first. The #196 line made up the balance of the order, which would be shipped over a period of time. The orders were shipped from Hamburg by Szenkovits Limited, a forwarding company, and started arriving in 1948. As requested, the orders for the #73 and #85 lines arrived first. All were very well made.

However, when the orders for the #196 line started to appear it was a different situation. The footed tumblers and footed juice glasses were according to specifications, but the items with stems were a disaster. With the "flared" shape of the bowl on the #196 stemmed items, the length of the stem is critical to the uniformity of the size of the bowl and diameter of the rim. These shipments had items with various lengths of stems. As a result, long stem sherbets had small narrow bowls, while short stem sherbets had large wide bowls. Attempting to group the different sizes resulted in the selling of some large bowl sherbets as candy dishes, selling the properly sized items for what they were supposed to be and selling the balance as distress merchandise. Eventually, about two to three years later, Glass Export of Prague offered a $3,000.00 credit on any substantial order in the future, but that was a risk never taken. It was the end of W. J. Hughes' business with Czechoslovakia.

Most of the shipping of CORN FLOWER was still done by train. Customers were as far away as Reid's Jewellery in New Westminister British Columbia, and Thompson's in Saskatoon on one side of Canada, to Lanyon's Jewellery in Hartland, New Brunswick and Kerr's of Cowansville, Quebec on the other side of the country. Orders in Toronto, if they needed to be shipped, went by truck through a local firm called Murray's Express.

A customer could always pick an order up as well, and that was the procedure of choice for the five Ostrander brothers: Jack, Vic, Ken, Ernie and Neil, each of whom operated a jewellery and gift store in Toronto. The Ostranders were all raised in Redickville, back in Dufferin County, around the same time as Jack. This meant they knew many of the same people. They often sent their young great-nephew, Robert Dynes, to pick up their orders. Later in the 1950s he started his own jewellery and gift business on Bayview Avenue in Leaside, where he, too, sold CORN FLOWER products.

A Wedding In the Family

PERHAPS THE MOST SIGNIFICANT EVENT FOR W. J. HUGHES AND SONS happened during the war. It was the marriage of Jack and Hazel's daughter, Lois, to a young RCAF pilot from British Columbia. Named Phillip Charles Kayser, everyone called him "Pete." It was Lois' cousin Don Kelly, stationed at Camp Borden, who had introduced Lois and Pete to each other in 1942. Don and Pete had known each other before the war, both growing up in Quesnel, British Columbia. On September 2, 1944, Lois and Pete were married in the Reorganized Church of Jesus Christ of Latter Day Saints, located on Bathurst Street south of St. Clair in Toronto. The wedding was much to the delight of her parents. Not unexpectedly, CORN FLOWER glasses were used to toast the new bride and groom at the reception held at the family home, following dinner at the church.

After the war ended, Pete worked full time as a glass cutter until the spring of 1946. Wanting to complete his university entrance exams, he was accepted into a rehabilitation school[22] in Toronto, where students upgraded their academic levels to prepare for university. In Pete's case, British Columbia's educational system had grade 12 while Ontario required Grade 13 for university entrance. Once completed, Pete returned to the Company, working as a glass cutter until he entered the University of Toronto in the fall.

Phillip Charles "Pete" Kayser

In 1944, Lois June Hughes married Phillip Charles "Pete" Kayser, a RCAF pilot instructor from Quesnel, British Columbia. Pete would take over the W. J. Hughes "Corn Flower" Company in 1951 when his father-in-law died.

A WEDDING IN THE FAMILY

A New Partnership

In 1946, Bob Hughes died suddenly of a heart attack. Jack was devastated by the loss, but also concerned about his ability to keep the business going, always being aware of his own heart ailment. His thoughts turned to his new son-in-law. Pete was young, had mathematical skills and some experience in the company. For his part, however, Pete was aware that family members in the same business could mean trouble, and Jack was certainly a very strong-willed man. However, he agreed to leave university and join his father-in-law on a full-time basis. In 1948, Jack formed a partnership with his wife, Hazel Hughes, and Pete Kayser, but kept controlling interest of the company for himself.

In forming the partnership, Jack agreed to have a factory building constructed on a lot he owned at 148 Kenwood Avenue, one block east and one block north of his home on Wychwood Avenue. At the rear of this lot was a large cement block, one-storey storage shed where he kept his European stemware blanks. Construction of a three-story cement block and brick building was started in front of the shed in 1949 and completed later that same year. One side of the building ran along a laneway just below Vaughan Road.

From 1912 to 1949, a total of thirty-seven years, all CORN FLOWER products had been cut in the basement of the Wychwood home. Now things were changing. Pete designed, and had built for the plant, a new and more efficient type of cutting frame. Each frame had its own electric motor providing power for each cutting frame as a unit, rather than several cutting frames being connected to a single line shaft by individual

Hughes family portrait (1947) taken at 212 Wychwood. From left to right: John Hughes, Lois (Hughes) Kayser, W.J. "Jack" Hughes, Graham Hughes, "Pete" Kayser. Seated in front is Hazel Hughes.

belts. Also, the new design required one-third of the floor space needed for the old type frames. A water drain was run from each cutting frame to a main drain, eliminating hand bailing of the used water required to cool the cutting wheels and to collect the ground glass residue formed by the grinding of the glass. This paste of glass residue was collected and dumped. A production line, consisting of one continuous table, was installed between two rows of eight cutting frames. Glass in process could now be passed from one cutter to another, without having to leave the work area, thus bringing nonproductive time to a minimum. Conveyor tracks were used to move blanks and finished CORN FLOWER products. Pete's new design increased the number of cutting frames to 16, whereas before only eight could fit productively in the basement at the house. From this point on, CORN FLOWER was no longer cut at Wychwood. The business could now expand. Storage of "turn lots" blanks and cut inventory was no longer a problem. Now a minimum shipment for one stemware item could be between 600 and 1200 pieces, depending on the quantity produced by one glass shop in the factory during a half-day shift.

At first the new son-in-law had to get used to the business ways and habits of Jack. Because Pete had worked in the factory, the employees liked him and they were willing to go the extra mile for him. Jack, however, was a workaholic and worked day and night. He had the same expectations for everyone who worked for him, even if that someone had a new wife at home. His two sons, both under ten years of age, were growing fast and strong. His business was going well and life for Jack was comfortable. W. J. Hughes and Sons had become a success story.

The staff of W. J. Hughes and Sons at 212 Wychwood Avenue, Toronto in September 1949. Back row (l-r): Bill Curtis, Bill Merkley, Bud Peace, Mike Graz, W. J. "Jack" Hughes holding grandson, Graham Kayser, Ernie McAdam, Bill Bayes. Front row (l-r): Bill McAdam, Jack Breathet, unknown, Lloyd Hughes.

Below: The factory and office staff in 1950 are shown with W. J. Hughes at the new Kenwood plant. He is standing in the back row, extreme right, wearing his familiar cutting apron and tie.

Prosperous Times

Over the two years that Jack and Pete continued to work together, they expanded business opportunities. Their new idea had been to promote the concept of a product line of open stock items from which customers could choose new complementary pieces or replace broken tableware without a problem. Corn Flower products were available in the local gift and jewellery stores, as well as from some of the large department chains. However, sometime in the 1930s, Jack had a disagreement with the principal buyer for the glass and china department at Eaton's. Consequently, the store stopped carrying Corn Flower products for about twenty years.

With the open stock approach in place, Corn Flower could be given as gifts, always with the assurance that the item would match the recipient's set. The practice of entertaining was being popularized by the leading women's magazines of the period. It was an era when a woman's social status was in some measure determined by her entertaining skills and sense of modern design. Women were encouraged to develop a "look" for their table to somehow keep their friends and family happy. With increased entertaining in the homes, there was a corresponding greater demand for stemware and serving pieces. Corn Flower prospered even more.

When Jack Hughes had approached his lawyer about setting up a partnership, his lawyer recommended that Jack consider incorporating as a private company, where he could control the company through the ownership of shares. While not initially accepting the suggestion, Jack

had agreed to give the idea of incorporation serious thought. His lawyer, his auditor, his bank manager, his wife and his son-in-law, Pete, all urged him to do so. Finally, in 1950, Jack capitulated and asked his lawyer to give him the details of such a step. After further discussions, the company was incorporated as W. J. Hughes and Sons "Corn Flower" Limited. The company was formed in 1951 with officers; W. J. Hughes, President; Hazel Hughes, Vice President; Phillip Kayser, Secretary-Treasurer; Lois Kayser, Director; F. J. McRae, Director.[23]

An advertising photograph, circa 1945. The first CORN FLOWER label is displayed in the front. After 1950 the corners of the label changed to a rounded, almost floral look.

The End of an Era

UNEXPECTEDLY, JACK HUGHES DIED OF A HEART ATTACK ON APRIL 17, 1951, at the age of 70. He was napping after supper with his three-and-a-half-year-old grandson Graham John in his arms. Always punctual with his bills, only four days before his death, he had written a cheque to Roden Brothers for $9.60 for silver-plated salt and pepper tops.

The funeral for Jack Hughes was held at McDougal & Brown Funeral Home at St. Clair and Pinewood avenues, in the neighbourhood where he had spent most of his life. Over 115 cars were included in the funeral procession and hundreds of people paid their respects. Many of Jack's faithful customers and friends had travelled from the Maritimes and from the western provinces to show their respect. Representatives of many of the American glass companies were in attendance. Imperial Glass was represented by Tom Ball, Vice-President and plant manager, and by Ed Kleiner. Jack lay at rest in the parlors in an open casket so all who wished would have the opportunity to make travel arrangements to come.

His body was interred in the Mount Pleasant Mausoleum in Toronto near his second wife, Annie. The sons Jack had so wanted were only ten and eleven years of age when he died. His son John was so very young when his father died, that when asked later in life could only remember with clarity his father as an old man who always cut through gas stations to avoid stop lights when driving. Neither Graham nor John were old enough to ever have taken part in the family business while he was alive.

In fact, they both chose other professions. Graham drove tractor trailers and John became a mechanical engineer and received his MBA in Business Administration. Until his retirement, he worked with IBM.

A local Dufferin County newspaper, the *Dundalk Herald*, printed this obituary:

> "A native of this district, in the person of William John Hughes, 71, [sic] died suddenly at his home, 212 Wychwood Ave., Toronto, on Tuesday, April 17. He was active up till the time of his regretted passing.
>
> Mr. Hughes, who spent his early years at Laurel and Riverview districts, was a son of Mr. & Mrs. H. Hughes. His mother passed away when he was quite young and he gave much credit to his father for his care in this motherless family. From a humble beginning in 1916, Mr. Hughes built up a successful business, which of late years has been conducted under the name of W. J. Hughes & Sons. At the time of his demise he was president. The firm which originated the cornflower pattern in glassware, recently built a new factory on Kenwood Ave. Originally the business was carried on in the cellar of Mr. Hughes' home on Wychwood Ave.
>
> Mr. Hughes was a man noted for his philanthropic work and each year distributed many hundreds of dollars worth of Christmas gifts, clothing and other necessities among poor families.
>
> For Riverview community, where he spent his early boyhood, a warm spot was always reserved in his heart and he took great pleasure in his visits there and put a high value on the friendships of his youth. From time to time he helped with improvement to the church there. He was a faithful member of the RLDS and a member of the Toronto Board of Trade.
>
> Surviving him are his wife, the former Hazel Graham, one daughter, Mrs. P.C. Kayser (Lois) and two sons, Graham Harrison and Robert John, all of Toronto.
>
> The Funeral was held Friday at the funeral chapel of McDougal & Brown, St. Clair Ave. West, and was conducted by Mr.

Booth of the Re-organized Ch. of J. C. Four Toronto nephews, a brother-in-law and a dear friend served as pallbearers. The service was largely attended. Among those attending were a number from Riverview district."[24]

In the "Riverview Column" in the same paper, the notation was made, "Mr. and Mrs. John Scace, Mrs. Lloyd Little, and Mrs. P. Markle attended the funeral of Mr. W. J. Hughes in Toronto last Friday."[25]

In the July 2, 1951, *Saint's Herald* published in the United States for the Reorganized Church of Jesus Christ of Latter Day Saints, the following tribute was paid:

> "William John Hughes 'Jack' as everyone knew him, came home from work one night and lay down for a little rest. He died almost as soon as he stretched out on the chesterfield. Every missionary for the last thirty or more years who visited Toronto enjoyed his generosity and hospitality. Brother Hughes was well known throughout all Canada for his beautiful Corn Flower cut glass. His customers reached from Prince Edward Island in the east to Vancouver in the west. A piece or more of his artistic handiwork on all kinds of crystal will be found in the home of almost every minister in the church who has visited Toronto. He was interested in people. His interest and concern for them was not just a Christmas time affair; it lasted throughout the year — especially if he heard of a family of children in need. Many acts of kindness were done by Jack, hence many rewards await him in that place where there 'are many mansions.' We extend on behalf of his many American friends our sympathy to his wife Hazel and their three children."

Shortly after W. J. Hughes' death, his son-in-law, Pete Kayser, as secretary-treasurer of W. J. Hughes and Sons "Corn Flower" Limited, placed an ad in the June 1951 edition of *The Trader and Canadian Jeweller*. It reads:

> "Originator of the world famous Corn Flower pattern, the late W. J. Hughes left behind him a tradition of fine glass cutting which is the exclusive and proud possession of our Company. Because of

this inspiration, this heritage, we feel that W. J. Hughes Fine Glassware is in a class by itself, and we intend to tell people so, from now on. We feel this is important to us, important to you. No pattern ever cut in fine glass has ever proved to be so popular as the Corn Flower which Mr. Hughes originated."[26]

From 1912 until his death in 1951, Jack Hughes had never spent any money on advertising the CORN FLOWER line of glass tableware in magazines or newspapers. In fact, the only type of overt promotion was CORN FLOWER being given as a prize at a charity fundraiser. The popularity of this particular cut glass was the result of word of mouth from satisfied customers or the suggestion of a merchant whom a customer trusted to sell a good product at a reasonable price. This glassware, seen and admired on many a table while being used, seemed to sell itself. Over the years it had become a pattern recognized across Canada, proudly carrying its creator's name: "Genuine Corn Flower by W. J. Hughes."

PLATE 1

Blue footed 4″ juice Tumbler;

Blue footed 5″ water Tumbler;

Tiffin #4194 crystal Jug with sky-blue trim[1]

PLATE 2

Tiffin #5001 sky-blue Sundae with underplate, c. 1925–1930

THE END OF AN ERA

PLATE 3

Tiffin #15033
Twilite Cocktail,
1928

PLATE 4

Tiffin #15024
rose pink Cordial
with original label

PLATE 5

Tiffin #336-2
crystal 11″ handled
Cake Plate;

Tiffin #020
crystal Table Tumbler
with gold trim

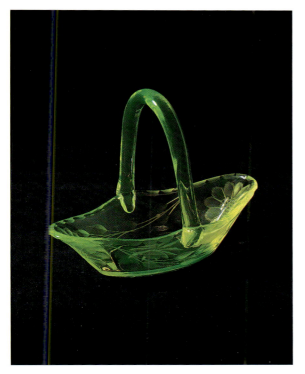

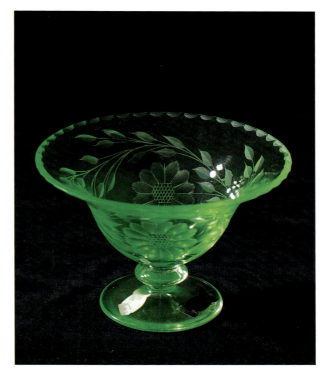

PLATE 6 (top left)

Tiffin #15151 canary Art Basket

PLATE 7 (top right)

Tiffin #320 reflex green Whipped Cream, c. 1925

PLATE 8 (right)

Tiffin #15011 crystal Goblet with amber trim;

Tiffin #15011 crystal Sundae with amber trim;

Tiffin #15011 crystal Goblet with green trim

THE END OF AN ERA   99

PLATE 9

Tiffin #101
green 3″ Candlesticks;

Lancaster #833
topaz 3″ Candlesticks;

Lancaster #355
green 3″ Candlesticks

PLATE 10

Tiffin #020
crystal Seltzers with
green trim;

Tiffin #15040
crystal Goblet with
green trim

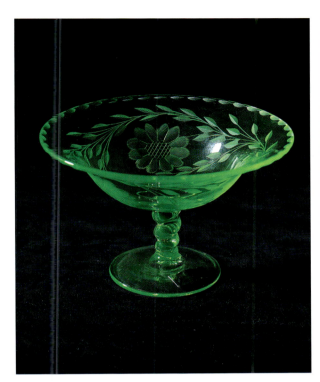

PLATE 11

Tiffin #315 canary low-footed Comport

PLATE 12

Tiffin #330 green high-footed Bonbon and Cover[2]

PLATE 13

Tiffin #14185 crystal Sugar with gold rim;

Tiffin #14185 rose pink Sugar;

Tiffin #14185 Mandarin Sugar

THE END OF AN ERA

PLATE 14

Tiffin #14185 rose pink Table Tumbler;

Tiffin #14185 lilac Table Tumbler[3]

PLATE 15

Tiffin #14196 rose pink Wine.

PLATE 16

Tiffin #345 pink low-footed Comport

PLATE 17

Heisey #1252
Twist (1928-1937)
flamingo 3-cornered
Mint

PLATE 18

Heisey #3350
Wabash flamingo
6" footed Comport
and Cover[4]

THE END OF AN ERA 103

PLATE 19

Heisey #1401
Empress sahara
10" Celery Tray

Heisey #1401
Empress sahara
13" Celery Tray

PLATE 20

Pink 7" 3-footed Bowl

PLATE 21

Lancaster topaz 9" 3-footed Bowl;

Lancaster T1831/7 topaz 10" 3-footed Tray;

Lancaster topaz 8" 3-footed Plate

PLATE 22

Lancaster T1831
rose 6" Rose Bowl;

Lancaster T1831
topaz 6" Rose Bowl

PLATE 23

Lancaster 354/3 "Jody"
topaz 12" Bowl;

Lancaster 353/1 "Jody"
topaz 7" Bowl

PLATE 24

Lancaster T899/4
topaz 11" 2-handled
Tray[5]

THE END OF AN ERA 105

PLATE 25

New Martinsville
No. 42 "Radiance"
#4227 blue 3-section
Relish Dish

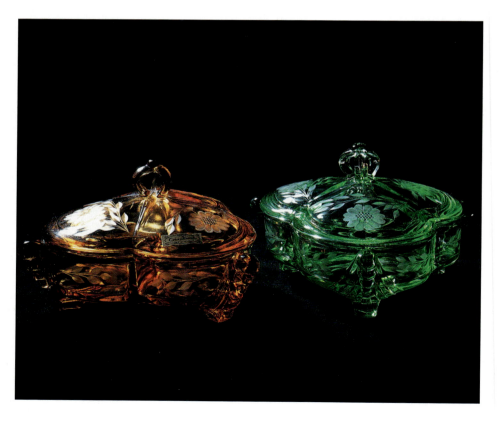

PLATE 26

New Martinsville
No. 103 amber Candy
Box;

New Martinsville
No. 103 green Candy
Box

PLATE 27

New Martinsville
No. 37 "Moondrops"
crystal Cream c. 1933;

New Martinsville
No. 37 "Moondrops"
green 4 oz Tumbler;

New Martinsville
No. 37 "Moondrops"
amber Cocktail
Shaker

PLATE 28

New Martinsville
No. 38 pink 9"
3-compartment Relish

THE END OF AN ERA 107

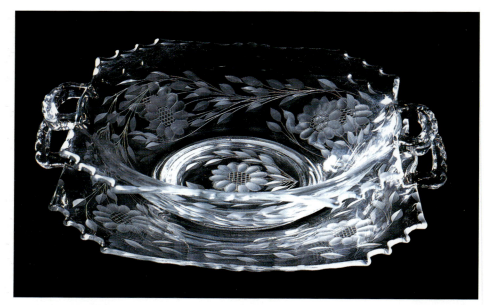

PLATE 29

Crystal 10″ 2-handled Bowl;

Crystal 10¾″ 2-handled Sandwich Plate

PLATE 30

New Martinsville No. 45 (or 4500) "Janice";

#4517 crystal 6″ 2-handled Nappy;

#4520 crystal 7″ 2-handled Plate

PLATE 31

Crystal 6″ 2-handled Lemon Plate;

Crystal 7″ 2-handled Nappy

PLATE 32

Pink flat Water Tumbler;

Crystal Sundaes with pink trim[6]

PLATE 33

Lancaster topaz Wine;

Lancaster topaz Sherbet with Sherbet Plate;

Lancaster topaz Saucer Champagne[7]

PLATE 34

Amber Cup and Saucer

PLATE 35
Amber 11" 6-part Relish

PLATE 36
Lancaster T885 topaz 11" Sandwich Tray;

Tiffin #330 rose pink 10" handled Cake Plate;

Amber 12" oval handled Cake Plate

PLATE 37
Crystal footed Iced Tea Tumbler with ruby trim[8];

Crystal footed Juice Tumbler with ruby trim;

Crystal footed Water Tumbler with ruby trim

PLATE 38

Crystal Saucer Champagnes with gold trim

PLATE 39

Candlewick-type amber 8″ 3-footed Bowl

PLATE 40

Crow's Foot amber 3-footed Bowl

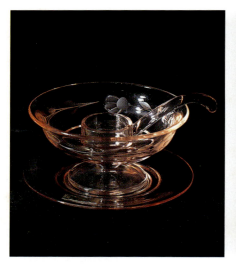

PLATE 41

Pink Mayonnaise Bowl with Underplate

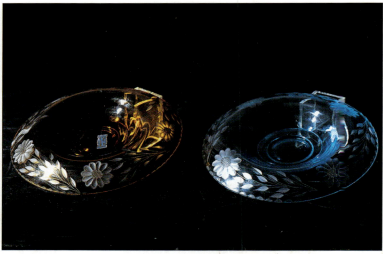

PLATE 42

Amber 10" Console Bowl
Blue 10" Console Bowl

PLATE 43

A variety of coloured round and octagonal Salad Plates

PLATE 44

Crystal Goblet with green trim[9]

PART THREE

The Kayser Years 1951–1988

FOLLOWING THE DEATH OF W.J. HUGHES, CONCERNS OF THE business fell to his son-in-law, Pete Kayser, particularly the need to determine if the firm could stay in existence without W.J. Hughes at the forefront. Fortunately, at Jack's wish, Pete had been more occupied in the administration of the business since it had moved to 148 Kenwood Avenue two years previously. Part of his involvement included dealings with the bank manager and assistant manager, as well as buying supplies and working with the office staff and the auditor. With Jack's assistance, Pete had been placing orders for blanks, and thus becoming better known to the glass salesmen and the glass factory personnel. With his experience as a glass cutter, Pete was quite aware of both ends of the business.

After the funeral, Pete's first move was to arrange a meeting with the auditor, the bank manager and assistant manager. Future plans and policies were discussed and, at the conclusion of the meeting, the bank agreed to back him and the continuation of the operation of the company. Pete's next move was to personally phone all of the glass factories that had supplied blanks to W.J. Hughes & Sons "Corn Flower" Limited, to assure them that the business would be continuing as it had in the past, with full support of the bank. He also wanted to confirm that any standing agreements the factories had with the company would be recognized and upheld; the potential of any misunderstandings in the future was to be avoided. During these phone conversations, two factories advised Pete, that they had orders being held, waiting for further instructions following notice of the death of W.J. Hughes. They now agreed to process the orders for delivery.

In 1951, succession duties were still being levied on estates, even when all assets were left to the spouse. The government appraisers placed high valuations on the investment properties of 214 and 216 Wychwood that Jack had owned. Over the years, these had increased considerably in value and were producing a small amount of rental income. While the company auditor felt that the government's valuation of the company shares was excessively high, he advised that fighting the valuation in court could cost more than what might be saved.

Hazel Hughes had lived in 212 Wychwood all of her married life and wished to remain there. As major shareholder in the company her husband had started, she too wished the business to continue. Seemingly the only way to pay the government succession duties was to sell the investment properties. However, selling the properties was not easy during the years of the provincial government's imposed rent controls which specified the amount that rents could be increased, unless an occupant vacated the premises.

When Jack bought 214 Wychwood in the early 1920s, a house was standing on the property. He had built a duplex in front of the house, and placed his showroom and glass museum in the basement level. Lois and Pete had been renting the house behind the duplex since their marriage. There was little interest in selling this last property until the realtor said he had a buyer, if there was a vacant unit available. With succession duty payment time close at hand, Lois and Pete agreed to move out to facilitate the sale of the property. This, however, meant that the showroom and museum had to be removed from the building. As showroom space had not been provided in the new factory, the CORN FLOWER contents of the existing one were sold to interested retail customers. Also sold off were black glass, china, porcelain cups and saucers and other various lines that Jack had attempted to sell during his years in business.

Lois and Pete purchased a small, newly-built house on Claver Avenue, in the Lawrence and Dufferin district, a location less that a ten minute drive from 148 Kenwood Avenue, and with bus service within two blocks. Lois and Pete's second son Christopher Steven was born while they lived in this home.

In the meanwhile, Pete soon realized that if the business was to continue to operate,[1] it must support two families but do so without the driving force of Jack Hughes at the helm. Something had to be done to increase the revenue of the company in order to provide for the welfare of Hazel Hughes and the two boys, and Lois and himself and their two sons.

Hazel Hughes, Life Without Jack

After Jack died, Hazel, at age 51, had to create and build a new life for herself and the two boys after having devoted her whole married life to Jack and to CORN FLOWER. With her husband gone, the two young sons had lost the influence of male parental discipline. This missing guidance became more and more obvious to Hazel Hughes. Although she tried her best at all times, she eventually recognized that the boys needed more routine direction than she was able to give them herself. Despite her best efforts the boys had developed a reputation in the neighbourhood for always being at the centre of trouble. After very thorough appraisal and consideration of what was available, she approached the Lakefield Preparatory School for Boys, located in Lakefield near Peterborough, Ontario. The boys were accepted and enrolled as residential students in this school, renowned for academic excellence and affiliated with the Royal Canadian Navy.

Throughout her adult life Hazel had never driven a car, but she now took driving lessons and obtained her driver's permit on the very first test. With this new-found independence, she could come and go as she pleased. Often she would drive to Lakefield to see the boys on weekends and on their "special parade" days. Sometimes she would pick up Janet Carr, her long-time friend, or another ex-nursing classmate or two from Grace Hospital, and they would have enjoyable outings visiting other colleagues who lived beyond the city limits. In time, she soon became an excellent driver and greatly relished the freedom afforded by the car.

For the rest of her life Hazel took very little part in the running of the company, although she was the company president until her death. She would remain at 212 Wychwood for many years. She preferred to let her son-in-law operate the company as she trusted his decisions, knew he was a good businessman and was very fond of him. Hazel enjoyed her sons and grandsons and played a major part in their activities as they grew, always being very generous with them.

When the family home was sold in 1970, she moved to an apartment near the corner of Yonge Street and St. Clair Avenue in Toronto. Unfortunately, a massive stroke in early 1971 would leave her paralyzed, and she was told by doctors that she would not recover. The indomitable Hazel proved them wrong, regained her speech and improved to the point of only needing a cane for movement. However, this restricted mobility was a devastating blow to Hazel as her whole life had been devoted to giving herself to her family and friends. Everyone who knew Hazel Hughes would agree she was a most loving and well-respected woman who did her best to please everyone. Her son-in-law, Pete, adored her. Hazel died September 25, 1974, less than a year before her first great-grandchild, Shawn, was born.

Hazel (Graham) Hughes' graduating class of 1922 held a reunion in August 1968. Hazel is in the back row, second from left.

Business in the Postwar Years

|T|HE YEARS FOLLOWING THE SECOND WORLD WAR WERE MARKED BY periods of unparalleled economic prosperity and growth. As the men returned and entered the workforce or the universities, the women returned to the home to maintain their role as housewives and to raise their children. Between the years 1946 and the early 1970s, the household per-capita income doubled, allowing Canadians to experience an incredible increase in their standard of living.

Following the war, the trend in society was to reject anything not perceived as modern. Old buildings were destroyed to make way for high-rise office buildings. Cities no longer were desirable places to live. With this new direction in development came the creation of "suburbia." Built on farmland outside the cities, suburbia represented "home" and "family" in many instances, concepts that many people no longer experienced. From the time of the Depression and throughout the war years, families had been split apart, and many young people had not married at all due to the economic and societal factors. Now, with the war over, these new subdivisions promised a safe haven for young families and housewives. Houses in the suburban areas were generally more affordable, allowing more middle income people to become homeowners.

One consequence, however, was that housewives often seemed segregated in these communities of look-alike houses.[2] Perhaps to break down some sense of isolation, the suburban lifestyle initiated a boom in home entertaining. Many of the new product items offered by CORN FLOWER reflected these modern times, especially the huge increase in the

The only existing invoice to a glass supplier from W.J. Hughes is this 1947 order for stemware to a small company in West Virginia.

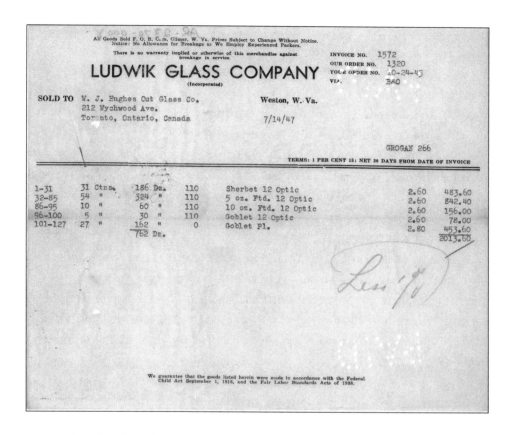

sales of cocktail shakers, martini glasses and ashtrays. CORN FLOWER, an affordable but elegant, cut glass pattern was readily available to the new young housewives. The uniformity of lines and continuity of supply provided young women the opportunity to start collecting their glassware sets, even before they were married.

In 1952, the year after the death of Jack Hughes, the CORN FLOWER logo, name and label all begin to appear together in advertising as well as on company cheques and invoices.

BUSINESS IN THE POSTWAR YEARS 119

Men returned to their role of breadwinner, while the women's role of being a good homemaker and mother was reinforced in all aspects of society and culture. Keeping an orderly and pleasant home looked good on the husband, as well as the wife. Retail business was good in the early 1950s. Canadians were making more money and, most importantly for the thriving economy, they were spending more.

Glass blanks were now readily available from the United States glass factories. And European glass factories were now looking for export business, wanting the United States dollars that they demanded as payment for their shipments. Blanks for cutting were plentiful in a market that was buying.

Pete was searching for ways to sell more CORN FLOWER products and to make the business more profitable. Concern for the price to the consumer had to be balanced with the need to cover costs and increase profits. Wages, taxes and other expenses were not lessening. Even though they were more readily available, the costs of glass blanks were increasing every year.

One partial remedy was to reduce the amount of cutting on a blank. While this option was not a welcomed solution, it did help to absorb some of the spiralling price of the blanks. This, however, was not something that could be continued endlessly, as a minimum of flower pattern had to be maintained. Collectors will begin to recognize the pre-1950s clear pieces by the abundance of cutting on the blank. Lower cost glass blanks were not an option if the high quality, a feature that had always been a requisite for CORN FLOWER, was to be maintained. Another potential recourse was to find blanks that would require less cutting and still be acceptably attractive to the consumer. But that "right" blank did not seem to be available on the existing market, so CORN FLOWER decided to make one of its own.

Pete approached a friend, Fred Myers, the Art Director and part owner of Walsh Advertising Company located on Yonge Street in downtown Toronto. When a good friend of Lois', Gloria Gibson, married Fred, the two couples became very close. In discussion with Fred, Pete explained the type of glass blank he was looking for and why it was needed. It was decided that Fred would create an eleven-inch plate to determine if something could be designed to meet Pete's requirements:

A 1953 flyer for wholesale customers of W.J. Hughes "Corn Flower." This advertisement featured Candlewick blanks from the Imperial Glass Company of Ohio.

SELL Corn Flower* OPEN STOCK

AND START A LIFETIME BUYING HABIT

The delicate charm of "Corn Flower" candlewick tableware captivates the heart of both giver and receiver . . . the kind of captivation that forms a lifetime collector's habit. Hence a single sale establishes two customers! Make sure you display prominently and feature in your sales presentation the fact that "Corn Flower" is open stock . . . then watch your customers come back for more and more.

EVERYDAY IS GIFT DAY FOR "CORN FLOWER" FINE CUT GLASS TABLEWARE ORDER FROM YOUR CATALOGUE TODAY

FREE NEWSPAPER MATS are available for use in your local advertising — more than 300 gift selections to choose from

GENUINE Corn Flower by W.J. HUGHES

53-4

*REGISTERED TRADE NAME FOR W. J. HUGHES & SONS "CORN FLOWER" LIMITED

The new "281" blank, cut with the Corn Flower pattern as shown in the 1953 catalogue.

two cutting areas separated by a simple design that would not detract from the graceful CORN FLOWER appearance. Ultimately, three designs were presented for selection.

Pete chose one that seemed to be most suitable for cutting and not too involved for the mold makers at a glass factory. The design had two four-ribbed swirls sweeping out in a graceful curve extending to the edge of the plate, from a double alternating row of overlapping circles around the base, effectively creating two areas for cutting. Tom Ball, Plant Manager of Imperial Glass Corporation in Bellair, Ohio, was approached and asked to look at the new design. How much would it cost to have molds made and produce plates and bowls? Tom indicated that Imperial Glass could make the molds in their shop at no cost to W.J. Hughes and Sons "Corn Flower" Limited, but production must be in "turn lots." The "turn" lot items from one mold could be made up of one or two plates and several different shapes of bowls. This approach would reduce their investment in inventory considerably.

More discussions led to a decision to make three molds for plates and bowls: one mold for a seven-inch plate, a six-inch cupped edge plate and two five-inch bowls; one mold for two eleven-inch plates and five nine-inch bowls and one mold for two thirteen-inch plates and five eleven-inch bowls. Molds for a two-section relish and a three-section relish would be made as well. The new CORN FLOWER line, given the designation of "281," consisted of 20 items. This is one of the few CORN FLOWER lines for which it is known exactly how many shapes were used, a bonus for collectors.

	The "281" line of Corn Flower
281/13D	13 inch flat plate
281/11D	11 inch flat plate
281/13V	13 inch cupped edge plate
281/11V	11 inch cupped edge plate
281/3A	11 inch crimp bowl
281/1A	9 inch crimp bowl
281/3B	11 inch belled bowl
281/1B	9 inch belled bowl
281/3F	11 inch shallow bowl
281/1F	9 inch shallow bowl
281/3N	11 inch cupped bowl
281/1N	9 inch cupped bowl
281/3W	11 inch flared bowl
281/1W	9 inch flared bowl
281/6	6 inch cupped edge plate
281/7	7 inch flat plate
281/5	5 inch bon bon
281/5A	5 inch cupped bon bon
281/2	2 section relish
281/3	3 section relish

As soon as Pete took over the Company, he began advertising in popular magazines. From the very beginning this advertising reinforced the expectation that all W.J. Hughes "Corn Flower" products should have the foil label attached before leaving the factory. This practice was to be maintained even on their own 281 line and on any other related products they might sell. Examples included:

- 1952 "Whenever you see this label you can be sure it's genuine";
- 1955 "When you insist on this label you can be sure it's Corn Flower";
- 1958 "Corn Flower Snow Flower - Look for the Label. Our registered trademarks are your guarantee to the bride that she can buy with confidence when selecting our stemware for quality and continuity. Do not accept imitations."

The First Corn Flower Catalogue

MORE THAN ADVERTISING WAS BEING REVIEWED. PETE DECIDED THAT more CORN FLOWER could be sold in retail stores from a catalogue showing the full line of available items than from a shelf of items chosen by the store owner. Once more he sought advice from Fred Myers and Walsh Advertising, knowing that this type of work was definitely in their field. The firm recommended the production of a prestigious catalogue that would present the fine quality of the glass blanks used for CORN FLOWER, with the elegance of the cutting clearly shown. It was believed that the quality retail stores which sold CORN FLOWER would be pleased to present this catalogue to their customers, thus allowing them to choose items the store might not have in stock. The selected pieces could then be ordered for the customer, without the store having the expense of carrying a larger inventory.

It was noted that excellent photography was the key requirement for production of a top quality catalogue. Without the clearest of images in the photographs, even the best printing company could not improve the look of the finished pages. To obtain the finest reproduction of the glassware and the cutting, the company chose Panda Photographers in Toronto. Their photography work with the CORN FLOWER glass provided truly exceptional results.

The next step was to select a printing company. Fred Myers recommended Brigdens Printers, also located in downtown Toronto. Here, copper plates were engraved for printing the photos on coated paper pages. The finished work had all the detail of the original

A sample of the exceptional photography work found in the 1955 catalogue. Imperial Candlewick blanks are featured in this shot.

photographs. It was suggested that each page have a reproduction of the Corn Flower label in a lower corner and that a 6-ring loose-leaf binder with a blue leatherette type cover be used to hold the pages. This would allow for the addition or removal of pages with ease as Corn Flower lines changed. In the centre of the cover was a large reproduction of the gold and blue Corn Flower label.

The end costs of the catalogue were going to be considerably more than Pete had anticipated. However, after discussions with Fred Myers, it was decided not to compromise quality. Fred described a very successful promotion his firm had completed with another of their clients, where the principal had asked his retail outlets to pay for advertising materials and the suggestion had been well accepted. Fred recommended that a small fee be charged to the retail accounts for the new Corn Flower catalogue. Pete, however, was reluctant to try this approach. None of the watch, jewellery or gem firms charged for catalogues, and many jewellers sold CORN FLOWER. Finally, it was decided that retailers would be charged five dollars for one copy, refundable on the first order placed after the catalogue was sent out.

Once the work order was signed, production began on the photography. The first true catalogue of CORN FLOWER was completed in 1953 at a cost of $15.00 each, plus packaging and shipping to the retailer.

Most CORN FLOWER retailers were delighted with such a complete list of items, all with outstanding visual representation. They used it to their advantage, often making additional sales from the pictures of the cut glass. A few were returned with comments such as "I have never paid for a catalogue before, and I am not going to pay for this one to sell your merchandise."[3] In time, many requests were received for replacement pages, frequently with the statement that the catalogue had been used so much the pages were getting dog-eared and torn. A few stores had to request an additional one because theirs had been left on the counter and had just disappeared. It was evident that the catalogue was being well-used. As new items were added to the CORN FLOWER line, new pages were made and sent to the retailers. When specific glass blanks were no longer available from the glass factories, the retailer or the CORN FLOWER salesman would remove the corresponding catalogue pages from the binder.

Today, original catalogues are rare and, when found, demand very high prices. To date, very few have been located. One, on display at the Dufferin County Museum & Archives, is almost complete. The products shown in this copy include 28 items of stemware, 99 items of Imperial Candlewick, 15 other items made by Imperial Glass, 12 items of the "281 line" (made by Imperial Glass exclusively for W.J. Hughes and Sons "Corn Flower" Limited) and 46 other blanks all cut with CORN FLOWER.

In later years, other catalogues were produced with Panda Photographers continuing to take the photographs, but the end quality of the finished book was much reduced. The pages were produced by lithograph printing rather than the more expensive engraved copper plate letter press. These catalogues were sent free of charge and, from time to time, new items were included in additional pages. Beginning in the late 1960s, the catalogue pages were printed in the CORN FLOWER factory, by their own staff. Currently, these catalogues are eagerly sought after by collectors.[4]

Selected photographs from the 1953 catalogue:

Fifteen-piece punch set: 6 qt. Bowl; 17" cupped-edge Plate; Cups; Ladle. Imperial Candlewick blanks.

12" centre-handled Pastry Tray; Cream and Sugar; 9" oval Tray. Imperial Candlewick blanks.

7″ divided bowl; low single Candle Holder; 9″ Bowl. Imperial '281' blanks.

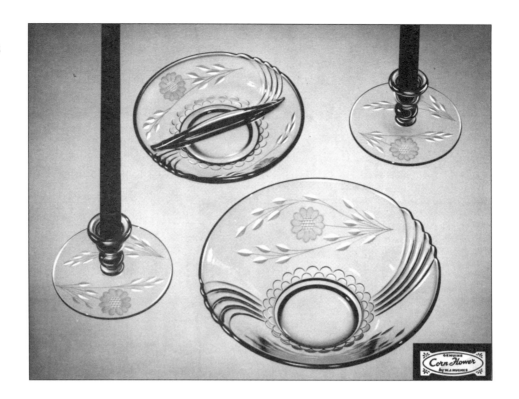

3 piece mayonnaise; 4 piece Salad set. Imperial Candlewick blanks

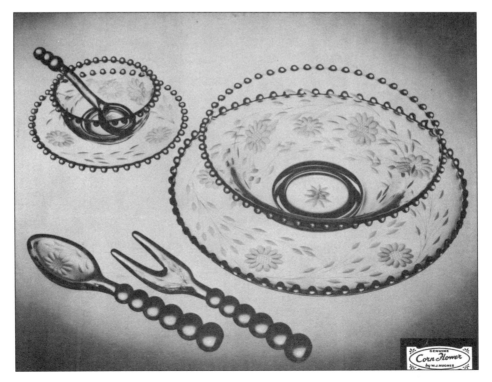

Two-tier tid-bit set; 6" handled Heart Tray; 5" unhandled Heart Bowl; four-piece Marmalade. Imperial Candlewick blanks.

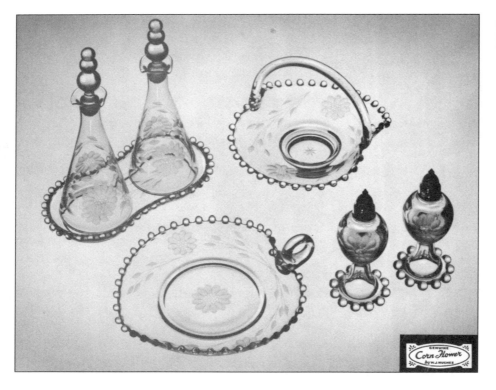

Three-piece Oil and Vinegar Set; 6½" Handled Basket; 6" Heart Bonbon; footed Salt and Pepper. Imperial Candlewick blanks.

Whiskey decanter;
42 oz. cocktail shaker;
42 oz. cocktail shaker.

Seven-piece Seasoning Set;
6″ Heart Bonbon;
5″ Heart Bonbon;
4″ Heart Bonbon.
Imperial Candlewick Blanks.

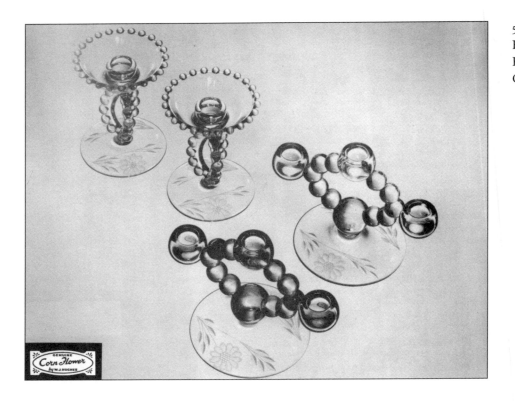

5½" single Candle Holder; 3 lite Candle Holder. Imperial Candlewick blanks.

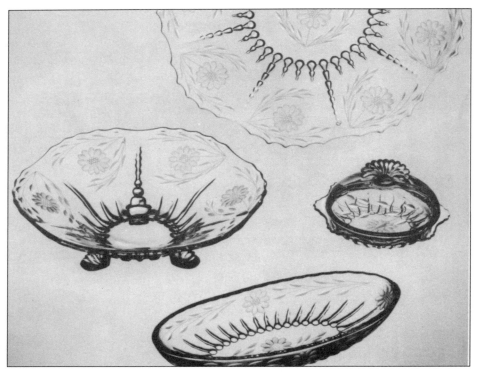

14" Hostess plate; three-footed Bowl; covered Butter; Celery.

Sold by CORN FLOWER as the 'Tear Drop' line, this was produced as 'Radiance' by New Martinsville Glass Company.

Production Innovations and a New Plant

I N THE NEW CORN FLOWER FACTORY AT 148 KENWOOD, GLASSWARE, whether cut or uncut, had to be moved from floor to floor manually. When a shipment of glass blanks arrived, the cutters stopped their work and carried the cartons of glass up to the third floor. When the glass was to be cut, someone carried the cartons of glass back to the first floor where the glass was unpacked, unwrapped and the factory labels removed. The glass items were inspected for quality, then carried up to the second floor in wooden trays. Here the glassware was cut, then replaced in wooden trays and someone carried the trays down to the first floor where the glass was washed, inspected, labelled and wrapped in newspaper. Finally, the shipper put the glassware in bins in the shipping room, ready to fill orders. In the cold weather, stemware, stored in the unheated concrete block shed behind the factory, had to be brought into the factory hours before it was to be cut, to warm up to room temperature. Obviously, the cost of moving glassware from floor to floor was a waste to be reduced as much as possible. One solution was the installation of an elevator or power conveyors. When investigated, however, the cost of renovations required to install this equipment was deemed unreasonable.

Not only was the movement of glass inefficient, but the company itself would have to expand to survive. With the recently built factory on Kenwood Avenue set in a residential area, occupying the total amount of land that could be built upon, space was limited. The solution now appeared to be the establishment of a new operation on one floor, with room for future expansion. After much discussion at the Board level, it was decided that Pete should work on a possible layout plan for a single-floor factory. The office and showroom could be very flexible, but the factory layout had to allow the processing of the glass to move smoothly from one stage to the next. All of the draft layouts were designed for approximately the same square footage, so a reasonably accurate cost for the building could be obtained. The final cost would depend on the value of the land purchased on which to build. When a realtor provided an appraisal on the 148 Kenwood Avenue property, it became apparent that the move to a one-floor factory was viable.

In 1952, the lot at 102 Tycos Drive in North York was purchased and plans were completed for a structure designed to fit on the lot. A building permit was obtained from the township and a mortgage arranged with a life insurance company. Once the factory and property at 148 Kenwood Avenue were listed for sale, construction of the new building began. The single story factory, opened in the late fall of 1952, was destined to be the home of CORN FLOWER for the next 33½ years.

With an area of 12,800 square feet, the building had two loading doors on the north side, one giving access to the shipping rooms where small incoming shipments could be received, but primarily it was intended for shipping goods out. Most shipments of glass blanks were received at the warehouse storage area and the cartons were unloaded onto the storage room floor, then sorted into groups. Once checked off against a shipping bill and the content count confirmed, the cartons were moved to their designated storage area by hand trucks. If large shipments were being received, portable conveyor tracks were set up in the warehouse and extended into the truck or trailer. Cartons were then sorted and stacked as they were taken off the conveyor track — all steps considerably more efficient than at their former site.

Two cutting rooms were adjacent to each other, with 16 cutting frames in each one. A concrete block wall built between the rooms, with open access at either end, was to reduce noise and limit conversations among employees.

Glassware for cutting was taken from storage by hand truck or dolly, to an unpacking bench located outside the cutting rooms. The blanks were unpacked, factory labels removed and the glass placed in trays which were then placed on conveyors entering the cutting rooms. As the cutters required glass to cut, the trays were taken from the conveyors and the glassware processed. The finished glass was replaced in a tray and placed on a conveyor heading to the washing, inspection, labelling and wrapping room. The wrapped glass was next taken to the adjoining shipping room, a space of 38 by 64 feet, in trays or wheeled carts and placed in bins ready for orders from the adjoining front office. The complete path, from start to finish was following the shape of a large "U." In the shipping room were three packing benches and a concrete block bin with fire sprinklers, for storage of packing materials.

At the front of the factory was the office area of 45 feet by 16 feet, plus a small private office for Pete. A short hallway connected the showroom to the office entry area.

The whole new venture was a model of efficiency for its day.

A Spectacular Showroom

THE SHOWROOM WAS THE EXCEPTIONAL FEATURE OF THE NEW plant. In the late 1940s, Pete had been to New York City to look through the showrooms of a variety of glass factory agents. During his rounds, he entered a showroom displaying lead crystal, a display so impressive that Pete never forgot the design principle used. Both the showroom and display stands were totally black and each item of glass was illuminated by a recessed light set below. When the overhead lights were turned off, the glass item appeared to be suspended in space, creating an unforgettable effect.

When the time came to plan for the showroom in the new factory, Fred Myers was called in once more. It was his opinion that a display company should be involved from the beginning, a move that would save both time and money upon completion. The three parties worked together in the planning stages. Recessed shelves would be on two walls of the showroom. The recesses were to be painted black. As Pete wanted these shelves to be illuminated in a similar way to the showroom he had seen in New York, he prepared a layout. Fred Myers drew a floor plan of free-form display tables with tiered free-form glass shelves to be in the centre area of the floor. A circular display case, with concealed lighting beneath each shelf, and a recessed rectangular display case, with fluorescent tube lights at the top and along each side, were placed in the floor plan. Groups of spotlights were mounted on the ceiling to illuminate the glass on the centre tables.

Once provided with this information, the display company made

The new showroom at 102 Tycos Drive, ready for the Opening Day in 1952. Even the curtains had the W.J. Hughes "Corn Flower" logo.

and installed the display sections, then painted the ceiling, walls and display cases. To achieve the special effect on the recessed shelves in the two walls that Pete requested, masking tape was cut to the size of the bottom of each piece of glass to be displayed. The tape was then applied to the underside of the glass shelving in a pre-selected place, and the underside spray-painted with black paint. Once the paint was dry, the masking tape was peeled off and the glass shelf replaced in the recessed compartments. Beneath the glass shelving was a double row of fluorescent tube lighting. When the lights were turned on, light projected through the unpainted spots on the shelves, creating the illusion that each piece of glass was itself a light, with the CORN FLOWER cutting standing out in relief.

A SPECTACULAR SHOWROOM   137

To further the dramatic effect, the single flower and leaf spray that was part of the company letterhead was enlarged and silkscreened in blue on the custom-made gold lampshades in the office entry and on the gold ceiling-to-floor drapes that covered one wall of windows in the showroom and offices. A large replica of the design was hand-painted by Fred Myers on a gold-painted wall, adjacent to the door that led to the adjourning stock and shipping room. Within the room, the use of curves on the free-form displays allowed customers to move freely around the startling displays of glass, set against a room alive with the vibrant colours of gold and dark blue.

The open uncluttered space and a modern look were the distinctive features of the new showroom.

The Grand Opening consisted of an open house in the fall of 1952 that lasted for two evenings. Every retail customer that dealt with CORN FLOWER was invited. All the food and beverages, catered by Canterbury Foods, were served in or on CORN FLOWER bowls, plates and beverage glasses. Lloyd Hughes, the cutting shop foreman, conducted tours around the factory, and some of the glasscutters worked late to demonstrate how CORN FLOWER was cut. Mrs. Loraine Taylor, who had worked in the company office for several years, was by then the full-time office manager with staff. She was there to help provide for the customers. Hazel Hughes, Lois and Pete Kayser, along with Fred Myers of Walsh Advertising and Charles Baker of Henry Glover and Company, Chartered Accountants, there with their wives, led the festivities.

The new showroom, one that many retail customers still remember and talk about today, was a major impetus for increased sales. Of all the customers who came to see the new home of CORN FLOWER, many placed orders in the new showroom and took their orders home with them from the stock available on site. But others came who were not customers of the company, including the president of the Toronto Dominion Bank and his wife, along with the manager and assistant manager of the local branch, also there with their wives. The whole event was recorded by the editor of *The Trader and Canadian Jeweller* who attended along with a photographer and a staff writer.

New Cutting Frames, New Cutters

WITH THE EXPANSION, NEW GLASS CUTTERS HAD TO BE HIRED AND trained to work the extra cutting frames. A few European cutters responded to employment ads, but most were cutters of window glass. The two female cutters who were hired, both of whom were excellent, paved the way for the training of more women.

Most trainees started by learning to cut leaves, a few began by learning to cut the petals on the flowers, but it would be four to six months before a trainee was producing well enough to be an asset to the Company. CORN FLOWER was cut on a production-line basis, so a cutter who learned to cut leaves became a specialist in that field. It might be several months before a cutter would be moved to another operation. Many practiced different operations during break periods or in their lunchtime. If they showed promise, they would be moved when an opportunity arose. Sometimes a cutter would be asked to try a different operation if there was a break in the production line caused by someone being absent or ill. The cutter would be supervised if he or she were new to the work, usually by Lloyd Hughes, Bill Curtis or Mike Gray. CORN FLOWER was cut under a pale blue light bulb, making the cut "stand out" more clearly, as it produced a pure white light and reduced the glare.

Along with learning the cutting operations, the cutters had to learn how to "dress" or shape the cutting wheels they were using for each different cut. The softer wheels, used for cutting leaves or petals, were shaped by holding a 120-grit dressing block on a steel plate, which was part of the cutting frame behind the cutting spindle. The dressing block

Cutting frame and wheels that were built in 1949 for use at the new CORN FLOWER factory at 148 Kenwood Avenue. These frames were much smaller and lighter than the older wooden frames that were used prior to the time in the basement of 212 Wychwood Avenue. This machine remained in use until the company stopped cutting in 1988. It is now on display at the Dufferin County Museum & Archives.

was rubbed against the face of the cutting wheel, to form the appropriate shape for the cut. Adequate water had to run on the face of the wheel while shaping it with the dressing block, to avoid overheating and burning the cutting face of the wheel, which, if it did happen, would result in scratches when cutting glass. When the desired shape was achieved, a fine 220-grit dressing block was used for a final smoothing of the cutting surface of the wheel. The leafing stone, or cutting wheel, sloped evenly upward from the sides of the stone, meeting in the centre of the cutting face. The shape of the flowering stone was convex. The degree of slope or shape depended on the contour of the glassware to be cut.

The harder cutting wheels used for spotting, stemming and nicking, required an initial shaping with a diamond dressing tool, then the same procedure followed with the dressing block as with the leafing and flowering cutting stones. The face of the spotting and stemming stones was shaped like an inverted "V." The nicking stone was convex with grooves cut in the face.

Moving the Business Forward

PETE WAS ALWAYS LOOKING FOR EUROPEAN SOURCES TO SUPPLY blanks for the three key lines of stemware. In 1952, a Mr. Houston and his son Jack who had a sales and importing business in Toronto, came to the Kenwood Avenue factory. They represented a company called Swedish Glass Imports and had received samples of a new stemware line the factory could offer exclusively in Canada. Pete was more interested in finding a factory to have the #73, #85 and #196 lines made, but this Swedish factory did not wish business that required the making of new molds as they used metal molds which were expensive to make. Their line of stemware was very different from the shapes currently being used for CORN FLOWER, but the quality of the glass was excellent. As well, the uniformity of size and shape could be assured since the stemware was mouth blown into metal molds. The company decided to try it. The new shape was presented as the #200 line, consisting of a goblet, a sherbet, a 5 oz. footed juice, a 3 oz. Wine, a 3 oz. Cocktail and a 1 oz. liqueur glass.

In 1952, Eaton's ran a newspaper ad for "Corinna" floral stemware made in Czechoslovakia. The stemware was an exact copy of CORN FLOWER! Pete spoke to the lawyer who handled CORN FLOWER infringement problems, and explained that he did not wish to antagonize Eaton's with legal threats, as he might wish to do business with them in the future. They had not done any selling through Eaton's since the late 1930s when W.J. Hughes had had an argument with the firm. The lawyer suggested that he might be able to handle the problem through a friend of his who was in the Eaton's organization. A few days later, the CORN FLOWER office received a phone call from A. R. "Bob" Prouse, department manager at the Eaton's Queen Street Store, requesting a salesman come to discuss the CORN FLOWER line. The end result was an arrangement; if Eaton's were to be supplied with CORN FLOWER, they would dispose of the copy immediately. Pete, however, was concerned about the reaction of the glass buyer at Simpsons' Department Store which had been carrying the line for some years, and was located directly across the street at the corner of Yonge and Queen. But after weighing all things involved, he decided to accept Eaton's offer. Although the buyer for the nearby competitor was most upset, Simpsons continued to carry the line. When he retired, his successor continued with CORN FLOWER until the store was absorbed by the Hudson's Bay Company in 1979.

In 1953, F. J. McRae, K.C., one of the original directors of the company, was appointed to a provincial judgeship, and advised Pete that he, F. J. McRae, must resign as director. Following some discussion, the Board considered Fred Myers as a replacement director in view of his qualifications and the interest he had shown in the production of CORN FLOWER advertising and the catalogue. Myers, on being asked if he would serve on the Board of W.J. Hughes and Sons "Corn Flower" Limited, agreed to do so, and remained for many years.

Retail Expansion

As production increased in the new factory, new retailers were sought to sell Corn Flower products. Frequently some, when prompted by eager customers, would ask to carry the line. Whenever possible, a Corn Flower representative would visit the store of a new potential account to observe the location and types of products carried and to meet the owner. Later, they would check out credit references, which within the trade were most critical to doing business.

Location was key to the selection of Corn Flower retail outlets. According to Pete, "A policy we try to follow, is one outlet for each 3,500 of population in a small town. In a large town or city, we try to keep our outlets at least two blocks apart."[5] Sometimes this was not possible, since other outlets might be just around a corner, or they could even shift location. Despite all best efforts, mistakes were made, particularly when the new account was in a town or city some distance from Toronto. This problem was greatly alleviated in later years when salesmen covered a territory, and were familiar with the setting of all stores within their area of responsibility.

From coast to coast, Corn Flower was available. In New Westminster, British Columbia, you could buy from either Eilers or Allen's Stationery on 6th Street. Small town stores did well with the expanding lines of cut glass. Retail outlets such as T.M. Palmer Jewellers in South Porcupine, Ontario; Parks Jewellers in Yorkton, Saskatchewan; D.C. Taylor & Son in Owen Sound, Ontario and Lavery's in New Liskeard, Ontario, all prospered from the expansion during the 50s and 60s.

New Ideas

I N January of 1953, Lois and Pete attended the annual Pittsburgh China and Glass Show, looking for new blanks and renewing acquaintances with the people from the glass factories. After completing their work there, they went to the Imperial Glass factory in Bellaire, Ohio. While going through the factory, the plant manager showed them several new semi-automatic glass cutting machines being used to cut tumblers. A tumbler was placed in a chuck (a type of holder) on the machine and held in position by pneumatic pressure. When a handle was tripped, the tumbler was rotated one position at a time. Once the tumbler was in place, a cutting wheel on each side would make a predetermined cut in it. Following the completion of a total rotation, the process would stop and the tumbler removed, to be replaced with another and the process would be repeated. All of this was being done without the need of an operator to do anything more than remove and replace a tumbler, thus allowing one person to run several machines at a time. After being cut, the tumblers were placed in an acid bath for polishing. The finished tumbler had the appearance of a lead crystal cut glass tumbler.

Interestingly, the manufacturer of this machine was at the Imperial plant that day and, following much discussion and explanation, Pete placed an order for one of these Walker cutting machines. These would have a part in the future business of the company, but were not used to cut Corn Flower production on blanks. Since W.J. Hughes and Sons "Corn Flower" Limited did not have an acid bath to polish the cut tumblers, Victor Walker, the inventor of the cutting machine, proposed using two brush-polishing machines to polish the cutting. One machine would polish with "Jeweller's Rouge," polishing out the rough grey surface from the cutting and the other machine would polish off the purple haze left from the Rouge with "Cerium Oxide powder." Both powders were used with small amounts of steadily dripping water.

A representative of one of the American glass factories who was quite friendly with Pete, was aware of how difficult it was to obtain a reliable supply of quality stemware blanks. On a trip to Europe in 1953, he made contact with a German stemware factory and became the Canadian representative for its products. It was his opinion that the quality of the stemware they produced would be suitable for CORN FLOWER. Upon return to Toronto, he obtained samples of the #196 line and sent them to the factory for pricing. As the quoted prices were acceptable, Pete placed an order for a turn lot of sherbets for a production trial.

The glass arrived in corrugated cartons, each piece wrapped in tissue paper. When the glass was inspected, the shapes and sizes were excellent, but many had a white halo band around the middle of the bowl. Pete called his friend, and several pieces were sent back to the German factory for inspection and comment. The initial response was noncommittal, but did point out that two factory executives were going to be in New York in a few weeks; they would come to Toronto to inspect the faulty shipment. They did so, but even though their factory name was on the cartons, they claimed that the glass was not from their factory. Neither did they know anything about the offending white marks. That was the end of that factory for both CORN FLOWER and the representative.

With hopes of salvaging as many pieces of the sherbets as possible, efforts were made to remove the white marks. Washing with soaps and detergents had no affect. Abrasives would not remove the marks. Polishing with a felt buff wheel and Jewellers Rouge, generally used to remove scratches and marks, did not work. After trying a mild acid bath with no result, Pete decided to send a sample to one of the chemical departments of the University of Toronto. Their explanation for the white marks was that either an incorrect temperature had been used in the tempering of the glass during manufacturing, or there had been some kind of chemical reaction involving seawater during shipment. The white marks were definitely within the glass and unlikely to have been caused during shipping, as the cartons did not show any water stains. The only process that had partially removed the white stains was intense heat with a high oxygen flame. Since nothing could be done, the Corn Flower company focussed its attention back on blanks closer to home.

During this period, the Company still cut on American stemware blanks, when and if available. Pete, exploring another possibility, bought a Pangborne sandblasting cabinet and dust collector for the purpose of frosting glass and sand-engraving designs on tumblers and ashtrays. The sales of these products, however, did not come up to expectations, but other purposes for the cabinet emerged over time. Business started to come in for blast-cleaning parts of cars prior to repainting and face panels for bank vaults which had designs etched in stainless steel sections. The largest job was the sandblast cleaning of VW Beetle engine blocks for the rebuilding of engines in the Scarborough plant, work that was a far cry from the original concept of the Corn Flower factory.

Changes for the Kaysers

After the birth of Christopher Kayser in 1953, Lois and Pete decided they needed a larger home for their family of four. They discussed these thoughts with Gloria and Fred Myers, who had twin boys and a daughter. The Myers who had been renting since their marriage now had desires of owning their own home. The two couples discussed their likes and dislikes and, following many lengthy conversations, became interested in the thought of buying land and building new homes close together. Finally, twenty-two acres of land in the Rouge Valley in Scarborough, along the Little Rouge River, were purchased. In 1954, each family moved into a new house, each on eleven acres of land. The Kayser home became well-known as the site for the annual Corn Flower Christmas parties given for their retail customers, and their pool was even used once for a Seagram's advertisement produced by Walsh Advertising.

Targeting the Bridal Market

IN 1954, W.J. HUGHES AND SONS "CORN FLOWER" LIMITED BECAME the exclusive Canadian agent and distributor for Imperial Candlewick and Imperial Vintage Milk Glass, a type of white glassware, often created in the form of punchsets, bowls, vases and other decorative glass. Some fine examples are on display at the Dufferin County Museum & Archives, courtesy of Lois and Pete Kayser.

With advertising known to have played a very important role in the great success of Candlewick, previously prepared copy in the form of coloured printing plates was made available to the new distributors. From the Canadian end, duty and sales tax had to be paid to the government on the cost of the preparation of the plates, but this was much less expensive than having the plates prepared in Canada. The advertising was aimed directly at the market of young married couples moving into modern suburban homes. One of the Imperial ads that they had used in the United States, was reproduced in the 1954 Fall/Winter edition of *Canadian Bride*. An article representative of the era stated:

> "On this day – her day – what better way to show how much her happiness means to you than by giving her something that will add to it in years to come? Her new career of hostess and housewife has a far greater chance of success when she can lay a table with elegant Candlewick glassware – always in perfect taste. Your favourite gift counter has a complete line of Candlewick Tableware – or they can get it for you. Place your order for her

happiness today! If your dealer does not stock your preferred item, write directly to us. Distributed exclusively in Canada through W.J. Hughes and Sons 'Corn Flower' Limited."

Another ad appearing in *Maclean's* that year went even further to emphasize that you could:

"...help a bride's career as housewife and hostess by encouraging her to choose the very best for her new home. 'Corn Flower' fine cut glass tableware gives her table that subtle touch of elegance her husband will be proud to proclaim. And your gift of 'Corn Flower' table pieces will add to a collection she will continue throughout the years, because exquisite 'Corn Flower' is an open stock pattern with more than 300 selections to choose from."

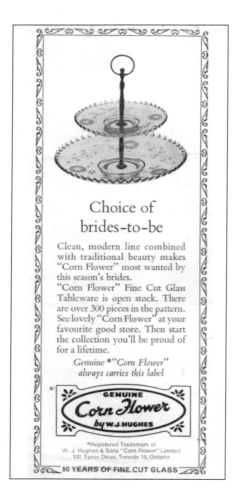

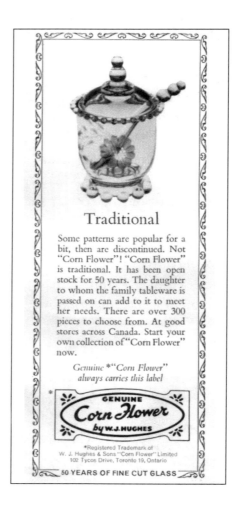

Advertisements in various monthly issues of *Chatelaine* in 1964 focus attention on the bride-to-be.

Brides were often targeted in promotions at retail stores, that carried CORN FLOWER. A letter from one of the winners from the Maritimes shows the beginning of the special memories that many CORN FLOWER pieces have for their owner:

July 5, 1958

W.J. Hughes & Co.
102 Tycos Drive
Toronto 10, Ontario
Re: Corn Flower Set

TARGETING THE BRIDAL MARKET 151

Dear Sir:

As a recent winner in Holman's June Bride Contest for 1958, I would like to thank you very much for the wonderful gifts which you gave to me through R. T. Holman Limited.

The pleasant memories of this Contest will certainly remain with me a long time, and I would like you to know that the name of your Company and its fine products will always be remembered.

Yours very truly,

Mrs. Arthur Andrew
(Nee Sue Jones)[6]

Imperial Glass Candlewick quickly became the top seller of the CORN FLOWER tableware pieces. In 1942, Jack Hughes had purchased $5,408.30 worth of blanks from Imperial Glass. Within six years, Candlewick orders totalled $15,218.08 and by 1952 the orders had soared to $54,682.68. Pete recalls placing an order with E.C. Kliener, Imperial's Canadian sales representative that year for a full railway carload of Candlewick. From Kliener's perspective, this was the first order for a carload of glassware that he had written in his entire sales experience. With the popularity of Candlewick, more than 125 different items were cut with CORN FLOWER at one time. In fact, over the entire Imperial Candlewick era, more than 200 different items of glassware were cut.

A representative of a Montreal trading firm, with worldwide connections, came to the CORN FLOWER office to see Pete in 1954. He said that his company had access to the stemware production of a factory in Belgium and that this factory could produce the exciting lines of CORN FLOWER stemware from metal molds and, as well, could guarantee size, shape and quality. This was the same old story that had been told so often, but Pete was still looking for a reliable source to supply stemware. A trial order was placed, and arrived exactly as ordered. This factory supplied CORN FLOWER stemware blanks for many years as well as the blanks for the "Snow Flower" line of glassware. As quantities increased, delivery time became more and more delayed. The last order received from this factory was shipped three years after the order date. Long before this situation developed, Pete was looking for another source of supply.

In 1955, a new special jet sandblasting cabinet was purchased to produce sandblasted images on glass through the use of specially cut-out abrasive resistant masks. Designs produced on glass included initials, crests, and motifs for bowling and curling. Combinations of crests and sports designs could be customized for club activities or prizes. Once more, the company was diversifying its products.

New Marketing Strategies

THE YEAR 1955 MARKED THE FIRST APPEARANCE OF CORN FLOWER in the National Gift Show, a show for wholesale buyers and associated trade attendance. Up to this point, the company had been concentrating on expansion, but now with exclusive rights to Imperial Candlewick and the Vintage Milk Glass, it was time to focus on marketing, The general public was denied admittance to the show as many exhibitors displayed their products with wholesale prices. By the time Pete decided the Company might benefit by participating, there was only one booth available, located at the back of the show floor. There was only enough space to display the best of CORN FLOWER products and some items of the Milk Glass line. As an introduction to this line, a 5-inch milk glass bud vase was given away to each customer who placed an order at the booth. Both Pete and a salesman staffed the booth when the show opened, but within an hour an emergency call was made to the office for help. They were flooded with prospective buyers. Consequently, printed order pads were placed on the display tables, and customers waiting to be served filled out their own forms, leaving them at the display for processing.

The show was not long underway when Pete had a visit from the show manager, informing him that items could not be given away at the show. Guards at the exit doors were instructed not to allow merchandise out of the building. By this time, several cases of the vases had been given out. Not wishing to cause embarrassment to customers at the exit, they decided to give a vase to each of the guards on the doors, allowing them to make identification of the giveaway. No more vases would be given out at the show, but a free one would be included with the customer's order. Before the show was over, Pete had booked four booths for the next year. As products were added over the years, the number of booths increased to seven as the standard reserved space for the company.

Following the success of the Toronto Gift Show, Pete thought a trial run at the Montreal Gift Show might be a good way to feel out the Quebec market, which up to this point had been little better than nil. Pete also hoped that the Montreal Show, being closer to the Eastern Provinces might give more exposure to the buyers from that area. The shows were held twice a year and were coordinated with the Canadian Jewellers shows, which were held in hotels in the cities at the same time. After two shows in Montreal, it was obvious that Pete was wrong on all counts. The Toronto Gift Show was the only show to be of value for the sales of CORN FLOWER merchandise.

Pete had many discussions with Fred Myers and the Walsh Advertising executives concerning the progress and the results of the advertising program. It was concluded that the limited amounts of funds being used for the purpose of increasing sales of CORN FLOWER would achieve more immediate results if they were used to advertise directly to the retail trade. This meant moving from the national magazine ads to the trade magazines. The new approach was to take full page ads to introduce new CORN FLOWER products and new product items.

To supplement and service their advertising strategies, the company had two salesmen in 1956. One covered Eastern Ontario, and made two trips a year through the provinces of Nova Scotia, New Brunswick and Prince Edward Island. The second covered Southern, Western and Northern Ontario.

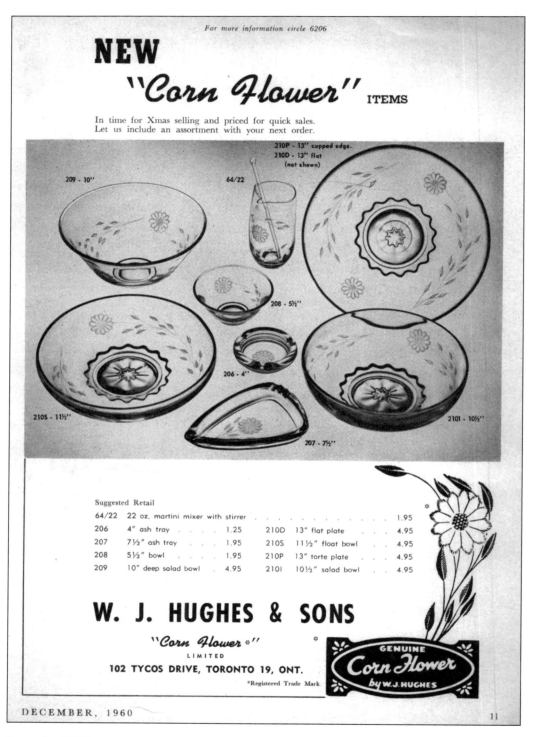

From the *Gift Buyer*, 1960

W. J. Hughes & Sons "Corn Flower"* Ltd. introduces attractive new decorator and practical pieces

158	286	284	285	187

283		301 (pair)	302

287 8″–6″–4½″–3½″	282	288

SUGGESTED RETAIL

158—Candy jar with cover	$1.95	287—8″ Ashtray		$2.60
286—4-piece candy jar set	3.95	287—6″ Ashtray		1.80
284—Hurricane candle holder, pair	8.95 (boxed)	287—4½″ Ashtray		1.30
285—Hurricane candle holder, pair	8.95 (boxed)	287—3½″ Ashtray		.90
187—10″ slant top vase	1.75	282—10″ 5-partition relish dish	6.95
283—6″ swan	4.95	288—"Princess" 8″ crimp bowl	3.95
301—"Princess" sugar / cream set	5.50			
302—"Princess" 10½″ celery tray	4.95			

*Registered trademark of
W. J. Hughes & Sons "Corn Flower"* Limited, 102 Tycos Drive, Toronto 19, Ontario

QUALITY AND CONTINUITY
GENUINE Corn Flower by W.J. Hughes
FOR 50 YEARS

JULY, 1964

64-8

23

As shown in the *Gift Buyer*, July 1964

This ad on the back cover of the February 1967 edition of *Gift Buyer* invites retailers to visit the Corn Flower booth at Exhibition Park in Toronto.

New People, New Products

I N 1956, A. R. (BOB) PROUSE JOINED THE COMPANY AS GENERAL Sales Manager. After WWII, he had worked at Eaton's as manager of the glassware department in the Queen Street Store. Very knowledgeable on various types of glassware, he had an ongoing desire to learn more. In a letter dated June 10, 1958, to Ed Kliener of Imperial Glass, on the occasion of Ed's 50th anniversary with Imperial, Bob wrote, "I have had 24 years of the glass business myself, and being human, feel that I know it all about the glassware trade, but I must admit, that in past conversations with you, I have picked up little things about the industry that I did not know formerly."[7] Throughout the years of working for the company, Bob Prouse kept scrapbooks of advertising, organized as to the types of advertising that had been produced while he was with Corn Flower. These books survive and assist in dating various blanks from their appearance in advertisements.[8]

W.J. Hughes and Sons "Corn Flower" Limited presented three new products in 1956. One was a lower priced line of stemware and tumblers called "Snow Flower," hand cut in the CORN FLOWER cutting shop. An advertisement aimed at retailers in the *Gift Buyer*, April 1957, stated:

> "Snow Flower…Created for family dining and large parties. When cost is a factor your customers will want this price wise line…it will cost them just $0.75 per piece, tumblers even lower. Created by this fine old firm with today's taste and young budgets in mind. Sample this line with your next order of 'Corn Flower'."

Regrettably, no authenticated pieces of "Snow Flower" have been added to the Dufferin County Museum & Archives collection. It is known, however, that each carried an identifying label.

The new Walker cutting machine purchased in 1956, contributed to the second new item. This machine could cut circles and spiral bands around tumblers. That same summer Eaton's advertised a sales promotion on a set of tumblers with a spiral cut design.

The registered trademark label used to designate "Snow Flower."

The third item was "Olympia," a line of lead crystal made in West Germany. It was very high quality, 30 per cent lead crystal, hand cut and beautifully polished. Each piece carried a foil label that read "OLYMPIA by Appointment to W.J. Hughes & Sons." There were two shapes of stemware and, eventually, 42 pieces of tableware. The tableware items included plates, bowls, sugars and creamers, cruets, covered butter, perfume bottles, atomizers, rose bowls, decanters and a large range of different types of vases. "Olympia" kept growing in popularity until the German factory decided to discontinue manufacturing tableware in 1970. Stemware was carried for a while longer, but without the tableware, demand for the line quickly diminished.

Also, in 1956, CORN FLOWER began featuring a range of products through joint promotions. The company supplied items as gifts for larger companies who, in turn, would then promote CORN FLOWER. During the summer of that year, Bob Prouse worked with the Canadian National Exhibition in Toronto for the CNE "Give-away-a-home-contest." The dining room table in the model home was lavishly covered with Candlewick glass cut with CORN FLOWER, the 18th prize listed was a 36-piece set of CORN FLOWER glassware and the company's name appeared in the thousands of free programs that were handed out to visitors at the exhibition. If a housewife wanted a dream home, obviously it should include CORN FLOWER.

For several years the program of display and giveaway advertising continued with the CNE. The women's division ran home decorating displays in the Queen Elizabeth Building and, in 1963, CORN FLOWER had nine listings there. The following year CORN FLOWER was featured in all

An advertisement for "Olympia" from the *Gift Buyer*. Produced in West Germany and distributed by W.J. Hughes from 1956 to 1970, each piece carried a W.J. Hughes & Sons Olympia foil label. The blanks for "Olympia" were 32% lead crystal.

"OLYMPIA" Lead Crystal - Exclusive with
W. J. HUGHES & Sons "Corn Flower" Ltd.

This top quality, hand-blown, hand-cut lead crystal line consists of complete stemware assortment, tumblers, sherbet plates and 39 tableware items. When you make your choice—choose the pattern with a personality.

Look For The Label

W. J. HUGHES & SONS
"Corn Flower"*
LIMITED
102 TYCOS DRIVE,
TORONTO 19, ONT.

*Registered Trademark

JULY, 1961

of the 16 rooms. In 1965, there were products in 20 areas but not in all rooms. Participation in the CNE displays continued until the 1970s when the show became known as the Home Furnishing Display.

The Viking Glass Company, in New Martinsville, West Virginia, in 1957, introduced the "Epic" line of glassware, an "Ultra-Modern" design, composed of free-form shapes of plates, bowls, relish dishes, bon-bons, ashtrays and candy dishes. The jugs and vases were "swung," making similar items slightly different from each other. With no pattern on the glassware blank, a substantial area was left completely free, thus allowing the cutters to enhance each item to the fullest, a feature that was most appealing to Pete. On the first order, every item that was suitable for cutting was ordered in case quantities. This trial order established exclusive cutting rights in Canada as long as volume of sales could be maintained. Pete remembers the gift show when the "Epic" line was introduced. Sales of the new line were so brisk that all stock brought in for the show was sold out on the first day. More blanks had to be ordered from Viking immediately.

The first advertisements to appear introducing the "Epic" line state "Yes…'Corn Flower'…known to customers for over forty years…now available in a new shape that is just made for contemporary living. The graceful lines of 'Corn Flower' blend ideally with a new free form style, in a line of nineteen pieces created for modern homes…"[9]

When Viking decided to stop making the blanks to bring out another new design, "Epic" was only continued in bright colours, none of which showed the cutting well and, as a result, was sold without the CORN FLOWER design.[10]

A whole new generation of young post-war families were buying homes and starting to entertain. At the first gift show in 1957 nineteen "Epic" items had been introduced. The line was so successful that. in the next year's show, eighteen additional items were added. Since stemware was not produced by Viking as part of the "Epic" line, the Company produced stemware called "Moderne," an elegantly flowing shaped line, to complement the modern glassware. When the "Epic" line was first introduced, Corn Flower stated the prices were "modest." A squared bonbon sold for $2.25, and an 18" free swung heavy-based vase sold for $7.95. "Epic" was an added line for CORN FLOWER and did not affect the

The contemporary looking "Epic" line, manufactured by the Viking Glass Company made its appearance in Canada in 1957. These blanks were cut with the CORN FLOWER design until the late 1960s.

sales and popularity of the top selling Candlewick line. Despite its early popularity, CORN FLOWER carried the "Epic" line for less than ten years.

The same year that "Epic" began, Bob Prouse wanted Pete to carry the Cutler Brand of decorated tumblers. Cutler Brands of Toronto had been producing silk-screened products, such as towels, shirts, caps, glass panels for appliances and many other products for some time. Now, having decided to try silk-screened painted designs on glass tumblers, they created some interesting items. Deciding to take the risk, Pete gave Bob "free reign" to select those he believed would sell well. Bob started slowly but, after some success, expanded the new line, making W.J. Hughes and Sons "Corn Flower" Limited one of the few wholesale distributors in Ontario for this line of decorated tumblers. The largest amount of business done between the two companies occurred when gift designs pertinent to anniversaries were made exclusively for the Hughes company.

The year 1957 also saw CORN FLOWER begin to supply their products to Canadian Armed Services personnel in the United States, an initiative that would continue right into the 1970s.[11] The following year, salt and pepper sets made in Japan and distributed by the Irving Rice Company of New York were brought in as a new line. While this line met with some success, the market seemed to prefer a different quality of glass

CORN FLOWER appeared in an Eaton's Christmas Gift catalogue for the second time, the first being in the 1930s. The 1959 catalogue featuring ten items. The ad copy read:

> "Sparkling Glassware by Hughes, with a delicate tracery of flowers, aptly called 'Corn Flower,' 78T 5¾" square bonbon. Each 2.75, 78U 6" Pair 3.95. 78W 9" three divided relish. Each 3.95, 78V candleholders, about 4" high, toed bowl. Each 4.95, 28 x 11" 3-toed cake plate. Each 4.95, 78Y salt and pepper. Set 2.95, 78Z Marmalade jar, cover, spoon. Set 2.25, 78AA 12" divided relish. Each 12.95. 78BB 8" bud vase. Each 1.25, 77CC sugar and cream tray. Each 1.50."

A copy of this 1959 catalogue page is included in the scrapbooks kept by Bob Prouse. In the margin are written the notes, "...one million catalogues distributed. Cost $1,350. Order for $13,750. 1958 Robert Simpson no ad copy order $2,800."

Although the comparison of the cost of advertising and the order for merchandise seemed to have been very profitable, CORN FLOWER did not repeat the venture. Since the catalogue ad was being prepared nine to ten months prior to being published, the price of the item had to be guaranteed for the time of the ad, which meant a year in the future. Delivery of the advertised items also had to be guaranteed and a provision for the unsold merchandise included. This arrangement was not as attractive as it appeared.

Television advertising was next. A flyer was sent to retailers for display in their windows. The copy read: "Corn Flower comes to life coast to coast TV, *Junior Magazine*, April 19, 1959. Check your local listing."

That same year, W.J. Hughes and Sons "Corn Flower" Limited became the exclusive Canadian representative for the complete line of Imperial Glass Corporation products. They carried stock of many of Imperial's products in the warehouse at 102 Tycos Drive, and distributed them to their own customers. Orders could be placed for direct shipment from the factory to the retailer or placed through the CORN FLOWER sales staff and sent to the Imperial factory for shipment. While this would bring the product to the retailer at a lower cost, it could be time-consuming. Most retailers opted to buy from the distributor in smaller quantities and avoid the problems of direct shipment. By now, CORN FLOWER carried plain Candlewick, Vintage Milk Glass, slag glass which was glass with no set pattern but carried multiple colours with one mold, End of Day Ruby glassware and a full line of Carnival glass, as well as other items considered to be saleable to the Canadian consumer.

Another product line also established in 1959 saw lead crystal salt and pepper sets, perfume bottles and atomizers, made by a glass company in West Germany, being imported directly from the manufacturer. The quality of the glass was excellent and the price, although on the high side, was acceptable. Unfortunately, prices increased to the point that sales decreased and the line was dropped.

In 1961, Viking Glass Company appointed W.J.

The personal touch had always been important to W.J. Hughes and the tradition continued. This 1959 Christmas letter was sent to all the many gift and jewellery stores that carried the CORN FLOWER line.

Three More Excellent Jeweller & Gift Store Assortments Priced for Volume Sales

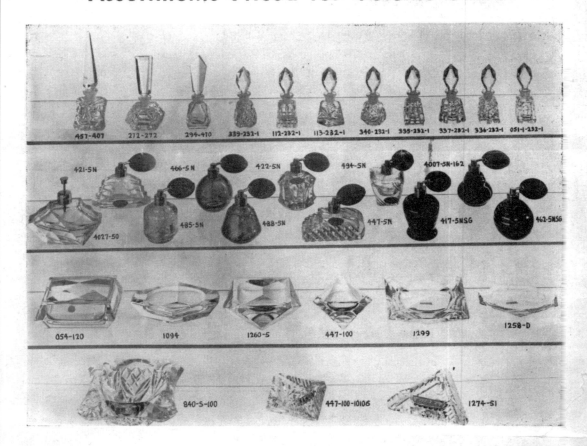

Cut Glass Perfumes (Ground Stoppers)—Can retail for $1.35 to $3.35

Cut Glass Ash Trays and Cigarette Boxes—Can retail for $1.50 to $8.25

Atomizers in Gay Colours—Can retail for $1.35 to $2.25

Available in early November just in time for Christmas sales.

Try an assortment of each when placing your order for "Corn Flower".

W. J. HUGHES & SONS "CORN FLOWER" LIMITED
102 TYCOS DRIVE, TORONTO 10, ONTARIO   RU. 7-1135

As the product line continued to be diversified in 1958, W.J. Hughes "Corn Flower" began to distribute these lines of perfume bottles, atomizers and ashtrays made by Fischer Glass Company of West Germany. No labels designating W.J. Hughes were attached.

Hughes and Sons "Corn Flower" Limited as their sole Canadian representative, with the exception of the provinces of British Columbia and Alberta. That year CORN FLOWER introduced "Visterama," featuring glassware combined with wood and brass, into the Canadian market. The glass was cut with CORN FLOWER while the wood served as handles and accessory parts such as spacers, and the brass was used for bases and fittings. The line had suggested retail prices as follows:

300	Trio party server	$7.50	305	Trio candelabra (each)	$7.95
301	Quartette server	$8.50	306	Cocktail tray	$8.95
302	Two tier tidbit	$7.95	307	"Vista" cheese & cracker	$9.95
303	Three tier tidbit	$8.95	308	Deluxe ash receiver	$6.95
304	Trio "Floating" tidbit	$8.95	309	Centre handle snack server	$6.95

In 1961, Fenton Art Glass Company was looking for a new Canadian representative. When they consulted with Viking Glass Company to ask who had been chosen to represent them after the loss of their Canadian rep, Viking told them they had selected W.J. Hughes and Sons "Corn Flower" Limited. Shortly afterward Fenton contacted Pete to enquire if "Hughes" would be interested in representing their company. After discussing this with Bob Prouse, who knew their product line and felt that it was one of the top glass companies in the U.S.A., Pete called Bill Fenton to say that they would be very interested in becoming Fenton's sales representative in Canada. The territory would be from Saskatchewan to the Eastern Provinces.

Pete and Bob agreed that the best way to sell the new line would be to do as they had been doing with Imperial and Viking products. This meant stocking items in the Tycos factory, for sale to those retailers who wished to buy in small lots. Direct orders would be written for those stores who wished to buy in larger quantities, with whom Fenton would deal directly for invoicing, shipping and payment. On these orders, Fenton would pay a sales commission to CORN FLOWER. The best selling items were selected and displayed in the showroom. Back-up stock was kept in bins in the shipping room.

W. J. HUGHES & Sons presents the
NEW... "CORN FLOWER"

VISTARAMA

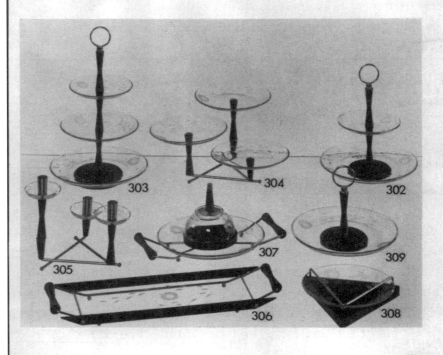

A brand new line of wood, brass and glass to give you an ultra-modern design enhanced by traditional "Corn Flower"

		Suggested retail			Suggested retail
300	Trio party server (not shown)	$7.50	305	Trio candelabra (Each)	$7.95
301	Quartette server (not shown)	8.50	306	Cocktail tray	8.95
302	Two tier tidbit	7.95	307	"Vista" cheese & cracker	9.95
303	Three tier tidbit	8.95	308	Deluxe ash receiver	6.95
304	Trio "Floating" tidbit	8.95	309	Centre handle snack server	6.95

W. J. HUGHES & SONS
"Corn Flower"*
LIMITED
102 TYCOS DRIVE
TORONTO 19, ONT.

* Registered Trade Mark

Another contemporary look for Coin Flower was added in 1961. This new line, combining glass and wood, was called "Vistarama."

Bob looked after the inventory and the ordering of the line. The sales of Fenton Art Glass products were gratifying, but with the advent of a listing under the Eaton's "supplier control" program in the 1970s, sales soared. Several years later, when the Eaton's glass buyer decided to carry only "clear" glass in the department, sales of Viking and Fenton coloured glass and Fenton Milk Glass slumped.

In time the warehouse became filled to capacity with a combination of inventory and sandblasting equipment. With new lines of inventory being added, storage space was urgently required. After looking at the cost of building an addition to the factory, Pete decided to purchase a truck trailer put up for sale by a transport company, the trailer no longer being roadworthy. Once a security alarm system was extended from the factory, both sides of the interior of the trailer were filled with glass, with an aisle down the centre. Eventually, there were ten trailers in the backyard, all of them containing stored glass.

The Rise and Demise of Aluminum Trays

IN 1961, A SALESMAN FROM SUPREME ALUMINUM PRODUCTS IN Scarborough proposed the concept of selling aluminum trays. They had a stamping machine to make the tray blanks, and had acquired a process for etching designs in the blanks which left the desired pattern with a shiny polished finish set against a dull gray background. The salesman, with his several samples of trays produced by Supreme, was looking for more distributors to sell them in the retail gift and jewellery trade. Both Bob Prouse and Pete liked the idea of the aluminum trays, but as Supreme already had several distributors, there would not be any exclusive position in the market for the Hughes' company. As an alternative idea, it was proposed that Supreme might make a tray carrying the CORN FLOWER design.

In due time a meeting was set to discuss the possibility of an exclusive CORN FLOWER line of aluminum trays. Supreme required artwork for the designs which they would transfer to their screening equipment. The items would be made in a required minimum quantity with the complete production purchased at one time. Once again Fred Myers was called upon to provide the artwork through Walsh Advertising. The result had the CORN FLOWER trademark design extended to cover the trays. On February 23, 1962, the first CORN FLOWER aluminum trays were sold.

These first ones produced included a 16-inch round hostess tray, a 13-inch round cocktail serving tray and 12 x 19, 10 x 17, and 7 x 15 inch oblong trays. The oblong trays had a metal trim edge with handles on each end. However, production problems with the metal edge meant changes in the tray were necessary. Finally, the edges of the tray were curved upward, eliminating the need for the metal trim, and also reducing the cost of the tray. The first trays were packaged in the boxes regularly used for Supreme's line of trays. At the beginning, these were fine cartons with a gold lid carrying the word "Silhouette" printed in black. CORN FLOWER later changed these to colours of silver and gold. Many retailers reported that not only did they not display the trays in these boxes, but when the trays were sold, they were placed in the retailer's own gift boxes bearing the store name. Eventually, CORN FLOWER had the trays shrink-wrapped in clear plastic for protection.

A small shipment of these trays was sold in the United Kingdom. Acorn Anodizing Company Limited of London, England, wrote to W.J. Hughes and Sons "Corn Flower" Limited, expressing an interest in becoming registered users of the design. They requested permission to produce and distribute the trays, but a patent application in Great Britain had not yet been completed, so arrangements could not proceed.

CORN FLOWER anniversary trays were added to the line in 1964. These oblong trays were a silver tone 25th anniversary and a gold tone 50th. The CORN FLOWER design was along the sides of the 17-inch width, with the anniversary year in the centre. The 13-inch round tray had the CORN FLOWER design around the outer edge with the anniversary in the centre, in similar silver and gold tones. Ultimately, a new crimped-edge round 13-inch tray was produced in the CORN FLOWER line for 5th, 10th, 15th, 20th, and multiple anniversaries, and also for the "Happy Anniversary" and "Bride and Groom" trays. All had a CORN FLOWER design around the outer edge with the anniversary designation in the centre, and carried the CORN FLOWER label on the back, along with the "Supreme" name.

In 1965, Cross and Olive and Pinwheel designs on trays were added, but they were slow sellers compared to the CORN FLOWER line. A tray displaying a group of Royal Canadian Mounted Police was introduced in 1971 to appeal to the emerging tourist industry. That year, as well, saw the last additions to the tray line of 13-inch round trays with trophy designs, two for bowling and one for curling. These became quite popular as prizes for members of clubs or groups.

In 1982, Supreme Aluminum Products advised that they would not

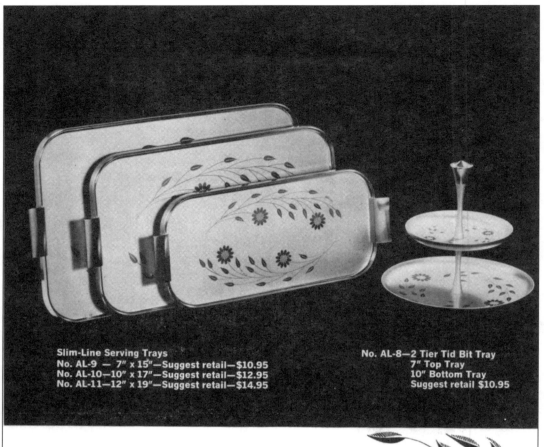

Slim-Line Serving Trays
No. AL-9 — 7" x 15"—Suggest retail—$10.95
No. AL-10—10" x 17"—Suggest retail—$12.95
No. AL-11—12" x 19"—Suggest retail—$14.95

No. AL-8—2 Tier Tid Bit Tray
7" Top Tray
10" Bottom Tray
Suggest retail $10.95

More News from
W. J. HUGHES & SONS "CORN FLOWER*" LTD.

Exquisitely gift boxed aluminum trays in the $10 to $15 gift class

*Registered trade mark of
W. J. Hughes & Sons "Corn Flower" Ltd.
102 Tycos Drive, Toronto 19, Ontario

QUALITY AND CONTINUITY
GENUINE Corn Flower by W.J. HUGHES
FOR 50 YEARS

be making any more trays. They needed the space taken by the tray-making machinery for an expansion of their cooking utensil division. They would make one more order for CORN FLOWER if it were placed immediately. Pete calculated what he thought could be sold in the next two years and Supreme was contacted. The order, delivered in January 1983, was sold out by November 1984.

In 1962, Supreme Aluminum Products located on Danforth Avenue in Toronto, produced ten styles of aluminum trays with the CORN FLOWER design for W.J. Hughes. Earlier trays were boxed, later ones were shrink-wrapped.

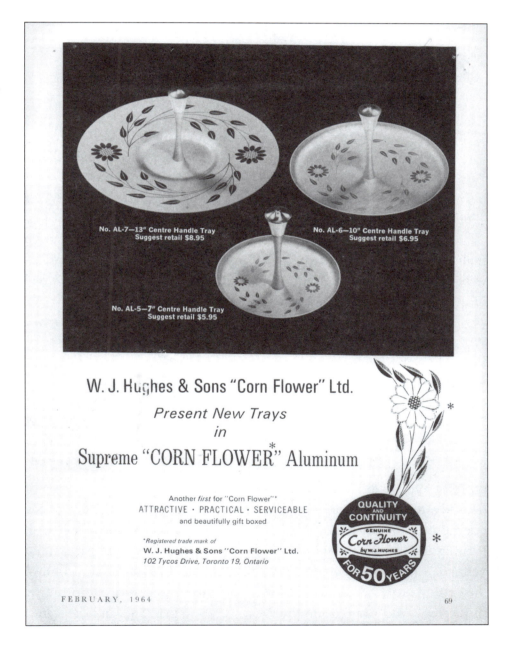

Premiums and Promotions

PREMIUMS AND PROMOTIONAL GLASS PRODUCTS STARTED IN 1953 with the acquisition of the first of the Walker semi-automatic glass cutting machines, and later with sandblasting equipment. In the beginning the Walker machines produced the circular cut "punty" or "Polka Dot" design, and the "Laurel Wreath" designs.

In 1956, Eaton's ran a special tumbler sale cut with a spiral design that "twined" around the tumbler from top to bottom. These tumblers were cut on a Walker "Spiral" cutting machine that had been purchased in 1955.

A promotional advertising company from Montreal approached Pete. They wanted to present a pilsner with a barley cutting to a brewery, for a company promotion to their distributors. Cutting the design by hand was too expensive for the promotion, but they had seen the laurel wreath cutting, done in a continuous band around an item, being sold at a reasonably low price. They had hoped that a barley design might be comparable in price. The barley design they desired was cut in a descending diagonal direction around the side of the pilsner, with the same design on both sides. However, the Walker machines were not designed to make this type of pattern and hand cutting was out of the question for the price they were seeking. Pete worked on the problem all evening and by two in the morning he had an answer. Special parts could be made to add to the machinery, which would change the direction of the cutting process and thus perform diagonal cutting. As a compromise, the barley "head" was cut on the Walker cutting machine, and the stems, leaves and whiskers were cut by hand. Samples and prices were presented within two weeks and the promotion was approved. Pete registered the parts he had designed, as a design improvement to an industrial design.

Another promotion was proposed in 1959, made up of two items of stemware and three sizes of tumblers. The stemware would be hand cut by a company in Montreal, but the tumblers were to be cut on the Walker cutting machines. Some hand cutting was added to the machine cutting to finish the design. The cut pattern involved a wheat head with a stem and some leaves on the stemware and the two larger tumblers, while the small tumbler had only the wheat head cutting. Production of these cut items had to co-ordinate with the packaging schedule of the product, which was washing detergent. Different items of glassware, in individual cartons, were inserted into different sizes of boxes of detergent. The "King" size box contained the stemware items. The "Giant" size contained one of the two large tumblers. The "Regular" size contained the small juice tumbler. In a production run the smaller boxes of the detergent were produced in larger numbers than the larger boxes, so the quantities of glassware varied with the different sizes of the product boxes. In discussions with the principals who were conducting the promotion, it was determined that the promotion should last at least three years. The Promotion Manager for the product stated the number of pieces that would be required in a time period. Pete calculated what the production would be per machine over an extended time. With two additional machines and crews working two shifts, delivery of the quantities appeared to be reasonable. Plans were made to proceed with the promotion. Two additional Walker machines were ordered and installed in the factory. Shortly after production of cutting had started in late 1960, the Promotion Manager increased delivery demand by 50%. Pete's response was to operate three eight-hour shifts a day. The promotion appeared in stores in January 1961 and, by early 1963, two additional cutting machines had to be put into production. Three shifts were operated seven days a week for over three years. In total, the Hughes' Company involvement lasted over five years. During this premium promotion period, the Company was employing up to eighty persons.

Bowlerama offered a promotion from May 22 to August 31, 1961, of five sizes of tumblers cut with a "Polka Dot" pattern: "One piece free with one fully paid game." A large pilsner glass was a special offer "Sundays only." For many years the Company supplied sandblasted design trophy glassware to O'Connor Bowl for their "Open" Championships. One of the favourite items was a pilsner with a gold rim and a sandblasted five-pin strike.

In 1962, Eaton's advertised a promotion of three sizes of tumblers, cut with an "Hourglass" pattern. These tumblers, cut on the Walker "Laurel Wreath" cutting machines, sold for $2.99 a dozen.

The following year, B.P. Service Stations ran a promotion of stemware with a hand cut "Leaf Spray" pattern. The promotion trial started with four pieces of stemware, at 33 cents a piece with every purchase at the station. Since the trial was successful, more pieces were added at 33 cents with purchase. Before the promotion ended, four tumblers, a sherbet and sherbet plate were included in the selection at 23 cents with purchase. Another gas outlet, "Johnny Martin's" Fina Service Station and "O'Connor Fast Car Wash" offered a promotion of a Walker machine cut pattern "Basket Weave" on a set of four sizes of tumblers "Free" with a car wash and $3.00 worth of gas, Monday to Friday.

Simpsons ran two sales on tumblers cut on the Walker machines, with a "Laurel Wreath" design in September and November of 1971. The promotion consisted of a 5 oz. juice, 7 oz. Old Fashion, 8½ oz. HiBall and a 12 oz. beverage. Each size sold for $3.99 per dozen.

The sandblasted "Crests" for clubs and organizations required very specialized work, sometimes involving the making of individual masks. Some clubs wished for a combination of their crest or logo with an activity motif, such as bowling or curling. Special customers included golf clubs, curling clubs, bowling leagues, private clubs, service clubs and hospital groups. Often particular "initial" combinations were requested, sometimes in combination with CORN FLOWER on one side.

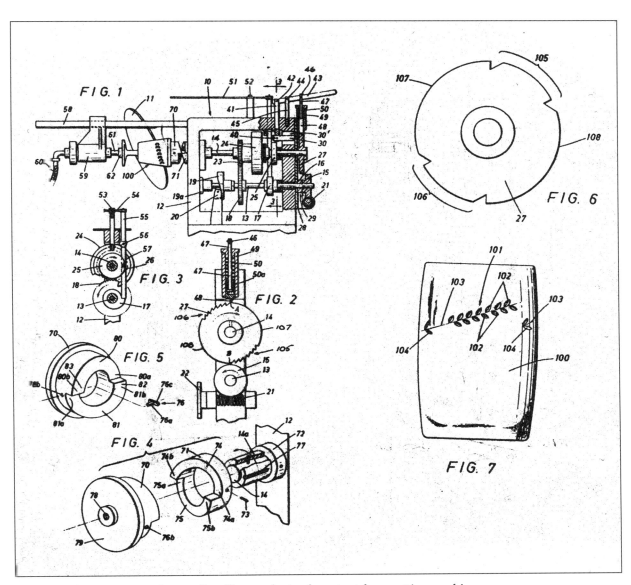

In 1963, Pete Kayser obtained a patent for a cutting machine.
The machine was used for cutting the "Premium" lines.

Open Stock and Quality Control

THE SUCCESS OF CORN FLOWER WAS BUILT ON JACK HUGHES' original concept of keeping the product in the medium price range. Effort had to be made to keep as many items "open stock" as was possible, a feat which was largely dependent upon the wiles of the glass manufacturer. In a 1966 interview, Pete was asked why CORN FLOWER was so popular. He replied, "CORN FLOWER is Canadian, is in the medium price field and, being open stock, is available for replacement". CORN FLOWER being "open stock" meant that a consumer could enjoy making use of her collection, knowing that if a piece were to be broken it could be replaced at a moderate cost, or on her next gift occasion. Any CORN FLOWER retailer could provide an item that would match her "set." The selection of gift items was almost without end, as new pieces were constantly being introduced. Buying a gift for a CORN FLOWER collector was as easy as going to the CORN FLOWER display at the local retailer, and looking for the newest pieces. At one time there were over 500 retail outlets across Canada that carried CORN FLOWER. Once a lady told Pete that before she married, she would allot a portion of her pay cheque to buy a piece of CORN FLOWER every month.

Selecting a blank to be used in the CORN FLOWER line involved two basic costs. The price of the blank was primary, to which was added the cost of the cutting that would be done on the blank. These costs, plus business overhead and selling expenses, produced an end wholesale selling price to which was added manufacturers sales tax. This was the price that Pete had to use to compare with any similar item presently in the line. A new item that was not similar would probably be on a trial basis, to evaluate the acceptance by the consumer.

When Pete Kayser chose a new blank or line, he always tried to obtain an agreement for "exclusive" cutting or selling rights for Canada. In order for this agreement to be worthwhile to both parties, some form of sales volume had to be maintained. Pete's thoughts were that, "if the Company could sell more of an item or a line as an 'exclusive' than could be sold if it were on the open market in Canada, then it was a good arrangement for both parties." If the item or line did not sell well, then it was not worth having as an "exclusive." There were no agreements or contracts signed for agencies or representative lines between CORN FLOWER and any other company. All agreements were by word of mouth and/or handshake. Exceptions were those products that were made expressly for the Company, such as Supreme Aluminum for CORN FLOWER trays, Cutler Brands for special decorations on glassware and ovenware, and Ferunion for mouth blown glassware cut for the Company in the Ferunion factory.

It was important that the employees became familiar with handling glassware. The glass blanks were inspected when unpacked from the manufacturer, checking for stones that might not have melted in the furnace glass batch, for air bubbles, or for chords in the surface of the glass. If a small flaw were to be found, it would be marked with a grease marker to bring it to the attention of the spotter who would position the pattern so the flaw could be cut out of the glass. A large flaw would cause the item to be put to one side so the cutters did not waste time on the piece. This took some judgment on the part of the person unpacking the glassware. After the item was cut it was inspected by the women who washed, labelled and wrapped the glass. It was checked for unfinished cutting, scratches and chips. The maximum acceptable loss through breakage and defect was set at 2%, as a hazard of dealing with a fragile product. This figure was rarely reached. The eyesight of the persons involved in the inspection process had to be keen since they worked rapidly.

European Sources of Stemware

PETE WAS CONSTANTLY SEARCHING FOR SOURCES OF STEMWARE FOR the regular CORN FLOWER line. Bob Prouse, the general sales manager, suggested that Hungary might be a good source, as he had been very pleased with the glassware received from Hungary while at Eaton's. With the agent for the glassware division of Ferunion, the Hungarian Trading Company for Technical Goods, being located in Toronto, access was simplified. Apparently the agent had contacted Pete some time previously, but after the unfortunate experience with glass imports from Czechoslovakia, Pete had been very reluctant to venture into business with Communist countries. However, he was now ready to reconsider.

In 1961, samples of the #196 stemware were sent to Budapest. Wooden molds would be used, so drawings of each item with acceptable tolerances specified, were sent to Ferunion, with a request that the stemware be made in only one factory. Once the requests were agreed upon, Pete placed orders for the first production shipment.

The quality of workmanship in the making of the stemware was excellent. The colour of the glass and the uniformity of size and shape were very acceptable. Even breakage in the shipment was negligible. The glassware was shipped in double-walled corrugated master cartons with single-walled cartons inside, each containing six pieces of stemware. The top, bottom and sides of the master carton were lined with a layer of wood excelsior for protection, as well as between the inner cartons. All things seemed to be too good to be true! Samples and drawings of the #73 and #85 lines of stemware were sent to Ferunion to have approval samples made. When these were returned, they too were as acceptable as the #196 samples had been.

At first, shipments were shipped within a year, but as quantities in the orders of blanks for CORN FLOWER increased, and as the European markets demanded more glass, delivery time lengthened. This type of experience had already led to the downfall of the business relationship with the Belgium supplier. Discussions were held with the resident agent and Ferunion's foreign representative, to determine the best way to avoid this lengthening of delivery time. The Hungarian representative suggested that if the Hughes Company made an agreement with Ferunion to supply the stemware with the blanks already cut with the CORN FLOWER design in Hungary, deliveries would be much more prompt. While this not so subtle pressure tactic did not amuse Pete, he knew that the prompt delivery of the stemware was crucial.

A few years previous, a buyer for a department store chain across Canada had directed stores to remove CORN FLOWER stemware from their shelves because the Company could not deliver wine glasses; they were "out of supply." The buyer's comment was "Stemware cannot be sold without wine glasses." Some retailers became most upset when their customers ordered regular open-stock items that could not be delivered, at no fault of the retailer.[12] The memory prompted Pete's response; if Ferunion were to supply the stemware, cut as samples supplied to them under an "exclusive license agreement" with CORN FLOWER, then some of the orders on hand could be delivered cut, as a trial shipment. The trial orders arrived and met with the approval of sales and office staff; more orders were to be delivered cut.

Eventually, an agreement was made with Ferunion; if orders were placed for stemware to be delivered two, three and four years in the future, and these orders were confirmed by the Ferunion office, then delivery would be guaranteed. This was placing considerable risk on Pete's shoulders, but delivery had to be assured as some CORN FLOWER retailers already had expressed dissatisfaction over uncertain receipt of goods in the past.

It was necessary, immediately, to calculate orders for the next two years and have the agent send them to Ferunion for confirmation. This meant looking through inventory and purchasing records. The usage of each item of stemware was estimated as if there had been sufficient inventory to fill the orders that had been received from the retail customers. These calculations, however, were being done before the advent of office computers, meaning that all projections had to be completed with pencil and paper and a calculating machine. Equipped with twelve column worksheets, Pete began his projections of stemware sales for the coming three years. Orders for the current year had been confirmed, but projecting sales for the next three years and backing the figures with orders was a nerve-wracking experience. Payment for the shipments had to be made in U.S. dollars, so foreign exchange rates played a part in the end costs when the shipments arrived in Toronto. Projections were rechecked each month and, if necessary, adjustments made to quantities and items on the worksheets. Changes to the orders for the coming year were made as necessary and several months ahead of delivery to ensure no disruption to the factory production.

The 50th Anniversary

T HE YEAR 1964 BROUGHT THE 50TH ANNIVERSARY OF W.J. HUGHES "Corn Flower." An aggressive advertising campaign was initiated, centred on a series of ads placed in *Chatelaine* magazine. Retailers were encouraged to advertise locally at the same time as the ads appeared in the magazine, to take advantage of *Chatelaine*'s promise that they would be sending the message to "over 1,600,000 English speaking women." A letter included in a promotional kit from *Chatelaine*'s advertising sales manager, A. B. Gardner stated: "*Chatelaine* readers are intelligent, modern homemakers always receptive to quality products and services. *Chatelaine* readers are able-to-buy women who easily can turn their desires into sales for you. Impress your accounts with the powerful W.J. Hughes & Sons "Corn Flower" Ltd. advertising being done to pre-sell their best prospects…*Chatelaine* readers! Be sure your accounts are prepared to meet the demand at the local level where it pays off."[13] To lead up to the year-long ad campaign, CORN FLOWER products had been used in several featured food article photographs in the November 1963 issue. Throughout the anniversary year, stemware was featured with very special prices, and promoted in the stores with special signs and promotional material.

The special, round foil label, with the regular CORN FLOWER trademark label in the centre, carried the words "Quality and Continuity" above the trademark and the slogan "For 50 Years" below. There were no special

The anniversary label was attached to larger pieces of glassware and used in advertising throughout 1964.

anniversary cuts or blanks. By the anniversary year, 50 years after its creation, CORN FLOWER had a salesperson in the Eastern provinces, one in Eastern and Northern Ontario, one for Southwestern Ontario and one for the Western Provinces.

A Response to Increased Cost

ON June 3, 1964, the United Glass and Ceramic Workers of North America, AFL-CIO, CLC, were certified to represent the production employees of W.J. Hughes and Sons "Corn Flower" Limited. Wages did not affect the increase in cost of producing Corn Flower, as the increases were less now than had been the norm before. However, the dissension between those who joined the union and those who did not created two camps within the employee group. Productivity decreased and tensions were high. Several employees quit their jobs, leaving for an environment with less tension in the workplace. The consequent reduction of production had a serious effect on the end price of Corn Flower.

Once again, Pete had to look for more ways to keep costs as low as possible. In addition to labour problems, the price of American glass blanks was increasing each year. By now, the Imperial Glass Corporation and the Viking Glass Company were making a large part of the Corn Flower line of hand-pressed tableware blanks, and products from other American glass companies could not replace these distinctively important blanks. One possibility, however, was to increase the range of Corn Flower items by obtaining more European-blown tableware blanks. The Ferunion representatives had left a catalogue of tableware items they could produce to order, but the orders had to be in turn-lot quantities. Many of these items were quite different from anything being made in the American mouth blown factories. Pete and Bob looked through the catalogue and marked items they thought would sell well

W. J. Hughes & Sons "Corn Flower"* Ltd. presents
PRINCESS "CORN FLOWER"*

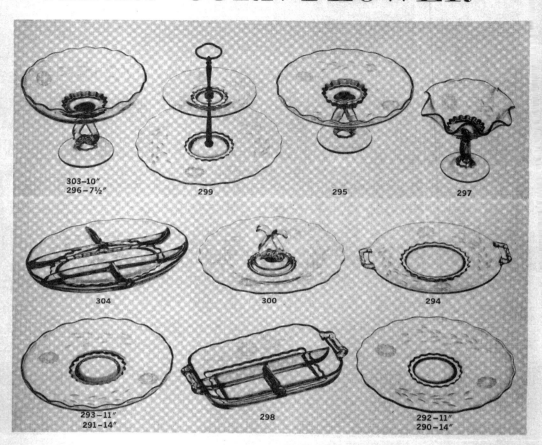

beautifully matched tableware to celebrate our 50th anniversary

SUGGESTED RETAIL

303—10" ftd. compote · · · · · · · $ 8.95	294—12" flat plate, 2 handles · · · · $ 6.75
296—7½" ftd. compote · · · · · · · 4.95	293—11" roll edge plate · · · · · · · 6.25
299—2-tier tidbit · · · · · · · 10.95	291—14" roll edge plate · · · · · · · 8.50
295—11" cake salver · · · · · · · 8.95	298—10" 3-partition relish dish · · · · 6.95
297—7" crimp compote · · · · · · · 4.95	292—11" flat plate · · · · · · · 6.25
304—13" 5-partition relish dish · · · · 8.95	290—14" flat plate · · · · · · · 8.50
300—11" tray, centre handle · · · · 7.95	(See No's. 288, 301, 302,—next page)

64-7

This 1964 advertisement in *Gift Buyer* shows the "Princess" line of CORN FLOWER. Produced at the Viking Glass Company, the design was cut on blanks dating from the late 1930s up to 1979. Many of the pieces are difficult to date as the same molds were used for many years.

enough that a turn lot could be ordered without too much risk.

In the summer of 1964, three men came to North America representing Ferunion. The group was composed of the representative who had called on CORN FLOWER previously, plus two export department men who did not communicate in English. The items of tableware pictured in the Ferunion catalogue that Pete and Bob had pre-selected for their meeting, created interest for their visitors. After an all-afternoon discussion and dinner, it was suggested that it would be in the best interests of the Hughes' company for the principals to make a trip to Hungary. A visit made to the glass factory to meet the management personally could be a good relations strategy. Pete agreed to give the proposal consideration, but in the meantime wished to see some samples of these items that had been selected. Shortly after the agents returned to Hungary, the samples, all of excellent quality, arrived in Toronto. The proposed visit was beginning to look like a possibility.

By 1965 the trip to Hungary to view the factory and, it was hoped, to place orders for delivery, was planned. Pete and Bob reworked the Ferunion catalogue and tried to estimate future sales. Since the visit had to be at the convenience of the representative who had come to Toronto, the only person in their organization who spoke English, the date was set for mid-June. Applications had to be filled out for visas to enter Hungary, passports obtained and the necessary vaccination and inoculations completed for re-entry back into Canada.

On the designated date, Lois and Pete, along with Bob Prouse, left for Hungary, by way of Montreal, London, Zurich, Vienna, and finally Budapest, a long, slow trip. There was a delay of over an hour in Hungarian customs, where Russian officers were the security people. Customs personnel peaked through curtains at the only threesome in the waiting room, and occasionally came out to ask the maiden names of their mothers or other seemingly vague information. Finally, they were released to the main airport where their contact was waiting, and he took the exhausted trio on to their hotel.

Along the route was much evidence of the recent Hungarian Revolution. Piles of rubble showed where buildings had once stood and had been blasted to ruin. Shell holes in the sides of buildings still standing bore witness to the fierce close-in fighting that had taken place. Once at the Duna Hotel, the registration clerk took their passports and advised them that these documents would be returned in a day or two. This news was most distressing, as the instructions given when the passports were issued in Canada, clearly stated that they should never be out of the owners' possession. Much later, they learned that this was a common practice in Europe.

The following day they were to go to the factory to meet with the management. Ferunion had three automobiles in their fleet. The car for the customers was a French "Prinz" and included a driver. Lois, Bob and Pete sat in the back seat, really only a board covered with cloth. With feet on the floor, legs against the back of the front seat, and knees under the chin, it was not long before the lower part of the body felt completely numb. As the trip to the factory took over three hours, the stop for lunch after two hours was very welcome relief.

At the factory, they met the management team and were given a tour of the facilities, including the cutting shop. Many samples of the blown tableware items that had been the main interest for the trip were on display in a special room, and even more items than had been in the catalogue became available. They talked about the stemware that was being made for the Hughes Company, again expressing a desire to cut the CORN FLOWER design tableware in their factory and shipping it as a complete product. Pete explained the problem of the extra costs of paying duty on the finished item, but this was difficult to explain through an interpreter. Late that evening, the party arrived back in Budapest and the representative took them to dinner at the Castle on the east side of the Danube.

The next morning's meeting in the offices of Ferunion was set to discuss quantities, deliveries and price. The representative was very co-operative. Stipulating minimum quantities for the items that had been selected and quoting prices, he then submitted costs for each item completely cut as the Hughes Company would have done it. All required recalculations, including duties and sales tax. The final decision was that the wholesale price to the retailer would be lower if the glass were to be cut in Hungary. Ultimately, a written agreement was drawn up, providing an exclusive contract between the two companies. The Hungarian factory would cut the CORN FLOWER design into the glass that was made for the

Corn Flower line, according to a license agreement. From the mid-1960s on, all the Hungarian Glass blanks were cut in Hungary before being shipped to Canada.

Once finished with business, and anxious to leave the war-torn country, they took the first plane with three seats available out of Hungary and found themselves travelling to Rome the following day. Bob Prouse stated that he "...felt more uneasy in Hungary than he had felt being a prisoner of war for three years in Germany."[14] It made sense that while in Italy, they would visit some of the world-famous Italian glass factories. Travelling by train, they went to Florence, Venice and finally to Milan for a Glass and Gift Show. After visiting several Italian glass factories, orders were placed for a selection of mouth blown glass, which included covered candy jars and boxes, decanters, wine sets, martini sets, cruets and many styles of vases some wrapped with brightly coloured plastic strings.

Two more business trips were made to Europe, one in the spring of 1966 and one again in the spring of 1968. On both occasions, Pete went to Hungary alone. During the 1966 trip to the factory, he was shown a reproduction of a #196 line goblet, approximately 15½ inches tall and cut with Corn Flower. An order was placed for a turn lot of these " display goblets." However, a problem for the factory was the great difference in the thickness of the glass between the stem and the bowl. When the goblets were put through the lehr for tempering, the thinner bowl lost shape before the thicker stem was tempered. The end production was only 100 pieces at a factory cost of $15.00 each; they were sold for display to stores at a unit cost of $10.00 each. The company kept several for showroom display and trade shows. Only two are known to remain intact today, one at the Dufferin County Museum & Archives, the other in the Hughes family collection. Others, however, may surface from private collectors.

On these same trips, glassware was purchased in Italy and in Spain. Also, orders were placed at a Portuguese factory, but for some unknown reason, the anticipated products were never shipped.

Canadian Design is Recognized as Unique

HE FOLLOWING ARTICLE APPEARED IN THE MAY 1966 ISSUE OF *Gift Buyer* magazine.

"Unique in Glassware"
By Rod Hanby

Unique is the only word that can describe Corn Flower. It was started in the basement of a home on Wychwood Avenue over 50 years ago and today is sold from coast to coast in department stores, jewellery and gift stores.

The managing-director of W.J. Hughes "Corn Flower" Limited, P.C. Kayser, tells me that the only way he can account for the phenomenon of the amazing, growth and continued sales increase, is that Corn Flower is Canadian, it is in the medium price field, and being open-stock, is available for replacement.

The basic glassware blanks are imported from the U.S.A. and Europe. Corn Flower is hand-cut by Canadian artisans in a series of five distinctive steps, the end result being a delicate and attractive product. It is handed down from mother to daughter and fits into the traditional or contemporary décor of present day homes.

W.J. Hughes "Corn Flower" Limited are exclusive Canadian agents for the Viking Glass Company and Imperial Glass Corporation. They are also Canadian agents for The Fenton Art

Glass Company, (excepting B.C. and Alberta)

Their general sales manager, A.R. Prouse, tells me that last year's sales of Fenton Milk Glass were the largest in the company's history. He accounts for this with the ever increasing demand in Canada for "Antique Type" glassware, especially in the "Milk Glass" field. This again brings you to the conclusion that modern and traditional are being used *ensemble* in today's home décor.

The sales on Viking Coloured Glassware also enjoyed a tremendous increase. This is a natural as Viking's colours are brilliant and beautiful. Having five distinctive colours, they can compliment any colour combination that is used today. The colours are Persimmon (orange), Blunique (a deep blue), Avocado Green, Honey (amber) and Ruby. The choice of styles are many and modern

Imperial Glass "Candlewick" is brilliantly clear glassware, with a series of glass knobs, or balls, running around the edge of each item. When viewed by candlelight, the reflections are extremely attractive. W.J. Hughes has sold Corn Flower on the large and varied assortment of "Candlewick" items for over 25 years and the demand for this combination has not lessened over the years.

Beautiful Corn Flower aluminum serving trays were introduced three years ago and Mr. Prouse informs me that sales are fantastic. Another innovation this year is Corn Flower ovenware for bake and serve entertaining, this again, a feature to compliment your Corn Flower glassware.

Although all lines, as mentioned above, are exclusive with W.J. Hughes "Corn Flower" Limited, the firm also handles other items, such as gaily coloured glass decorative candles and a large assortment of Italian hand-blown art glassware in Peacock and "Bottle" Green, Amber and Ruby.

In conclusion, they've something for all tastes in style and colour for the most discriminating hostess.

Gift Buyer, May 1966."[15]

Centennial Year and the Sixties

CORN FLOWER OVENWARE LINE WAS INTRODUCED ON FEBRUARY 21, 1966. This opaque milk-white, heatproof oven-to-table glassware was produced by the Federal Glass Company of Columbus, Ohio. Walsh Advertising, through Fred Myers, produced drawings to make transfers of the CORN FLOWER designs for the application and firing of blue paint on the exterior of the ovenware pieces. Cutler Brands Limited, the same company which began producing silkscreened tumblers in 1957, performed the application of the designs to the ovenware. Altogether, the line consisted of 10 pieces:

CF 50	3½ Quart covered casserole
CF 51	2½ Quart covered casserole
CF 52	1½ Quart covered casseroleb1
CF 53	8" Round cake pan w/cover
CF 54	3 piece Bowl set/1½ Quart/2½ Quart/ 3½ Quart
CF 55	Coffee mug
CF 56	2 piece utility set/2½ Quart/1½ Quart
CF 57	3 piece covered pan set
CF 58	Tea mug
CF 59	1 cup Casserole

The CORN FLOWER ovenware, introduced in 1966, was marketed as a gift line, each piece placed in an individual box bearing the CORN FLOWER foil label.

CF 50   CF 51   CF 52   CF 53

CF 54   CF 55   CF 56   CF 57

"CORN FLOWER" BAKE & SERVE OVENWARE

Every item individually gift boxed and bearing the familiar "Corn Flower" Label

		Net Price
CF 50	3½ Quart Covered Casserole	2.50 each
CF 51	2½ Quart Covered Casserole	1.90 each
CF 52	1½ Quart Covered Casserole	1.65 each
CF 53	1¼ Quart Covered Casserole	1.95 each
CF 54	3 Pc. Mixing Bowl Set (1½ - 2½ - 3½ Qt.)	3.15 set
CF 55	4 Pc. Coffee Mug Set (9½ oz.)	1.15 set
CF 56	2 Pc. Bake Set (1½ Quart Utility Pan) (1¼ Quart Loaf Pan)	2.60 set
CF 57	3 Pc. Cake-Bake Set (1¼ Qt. Covered Casserole) (8" Round Cake Pan)	2.95 set
CF 58	4 Pc. Continental Mug Set (8 oz.) (Not Illus.)	1.90 set
CF 59	4 Pc. Individual Bowl Set (5" Dia.) (Not Illus.)	1.20 set

Two year guarantee against normal oven heat breakage.
Not for Top of Stove Use.

*Registered Trademark of

W. J. HUGHES & SONS, "CORN FLOWER"* LIMITED
102 TYCOS DRIVE   TORONTO 19, ONTARIO

JUNE, 1966

Also released in 1966, this line of tumblers featured a frosted white band with the blue silkscreened CORN FLOWER.

On March 25, 1966, an agreement was made with Cutler Brands as follows: "We hereby agree that we will confine the reproduction of Cornflower (sic) on glassware, including ovenware, tumblers and all other items of glassware, solely to W.J. Hughes & Sons Cornflower (sic) Limited. This agreement also covers any reproductions on textiles such as towels, aprons, face cloths, etc. We believe this agreement should also work in reverse, i.e., W.J. Hughes would agree that Cutler Brands Limited would be its only supplier of the items, i.e., glassware or textiles, types which would be supplied by the silk screen decoration process."[16]

In 1967, Canada's "Centennial" year, W.J. Hughes and Sons "Corn Flower" Limited ran a sale. Special prices were offered and promotional materials, signs and advertising provided at no cost to the retailer. Regular stemware was discounted throughout the year and various items of tableware were offered at special prices. Some examples of prices are shown:

No "special cut" was made to celebrate Canada's birthday.

"Caramia" stemware and tableware, made up of mouth blown stemware and glassware made and cut in Hungary, were introduced as a lower priced glassware line than the CORN FLOWER design. The first sale of this line was on November 8, 1967, as indicated on Invoice #74867, to

2 handled cream & sugar	$5.25	double oil & vinegar	$4.95
30 oz. ice lip jug	$5.50	candy jar with lid	$6.75
10" trumpet vase	$5.95	salt & pepper set	$4.95
6" rose bowl plain top	$3.25	6" three toe bowl	$4.95
120 oz. brandy	$8.75	low candleholder (pair)	$5.50
shrimp cocktail & liner	$3.25	covered marmalade	$2.75

Hartley Jewellery of Waterford, Ontario. The name "Caramia" was registered as a trademark and the design registered as an industrial design. The gold and black label bore the name "Caramia," with the identification RD 68 at the bottom to indicate the design registration. "Caramia" was carried for ten years, by which time the costs of the items were comparable to those of CORN FLOWER, but sales declined to a point that did not justify continuing the line.

In 1969, a man came to the office with what seemed to be a new idea in the trade. He said that he had developed a process for photo-engraving pictures on metal and was presently creating early Canadian scenes on oblong aluminum trays which he was presenting as serving trays. The scenes were taken from an old book on the history of Canadian settlement and development. Since he was seeking a company to handle sales and distribution, Pete and Bob thought there might be a possibility for more sales. They agreed to buy some trays and present them at the next Gift Show. While several hundreds of the trays were sold over the following two years, sales were not as had been hoped and the product was dropped.

Another Kayser Joins the Company

G RAHAM KAYSER, LOIS AND PETE'S ELDEST SON, NOW 21 YEARS OF age, joined the company in 1969, and was the last employee to leave when glass operations were terminated in 1988. Beginning exclusively in the Toronto area, Graham was discouraged when he only received orders from a few Toronto retailers who were still catering to their loyal CORN FLOWER customers. After speaking with Bob Prouse, the two went out together to see if there was a problem with Graham's approach or with the CORN FLOWER product. After several days of calling on stores, they discovered that a great change had taken place in Toronto merchandising.

In the years during and shortly after the war, merchandise was in short supply and Jewellery and Gift Shop owners were looking for items to sell in their stores. By now, a large variety of merchandise was available to the consumers. Rents, taxes and salaries had increased from the earlier years, and retailers now required a greater dollar return per foot of shelf or display space to cover overhead expenses. Medium priced CORN FLOWER produced a medium dollar return, and required a lot of display space. Watches, diamond jewellery and rings, on the other hand, provided a much greater return from sales. Silverware and lead crystal took as much space to display as CORN FLOWER, but supplied more revenue because of the higher selling prices. If the retailer required CORN FLOWER for a customer, and had an account, all he needed to do was phone an order in to the Company office and it would be delivered in a day or two. The same conditions applied to all retailers of CORN FLOWER, but it seemed to be more pronounced in Toronto where salesmen were virtually redundant.

Pete decided that Graham's talents might be of more value to the company in other ways as he had taken a commercial course during his education. Although not enthusiastic about office work, he was a capable typist and had some bookkeeping training. The office manager agreed to accept Graham's help in the office, with the understanding by all that Graham might be moved around from time to time to perform other tasks. One day, while watching an order for a sandblasted design being worked on the small canister blasting cabinet, Graham expressed a desire to learn more about this seemingly more challenging operation. Soon he was doing most of the sandblasting design work.

For some time now the company had been using a department of the Gestetner Company in Don Mills to print price lists and order forms every year, as catalogue pages had to be printed whenever new items were added. Ultimately, business increased to the point that a salesman from Gestetner suggested that money could be saved if a fully reconditioned offset printing machine were acquired. Gestetner could "burn" the printing plates and the printing could be done in the CORN FLOWER factory. The machine was purchased and set up in the factory, with the office manager agreeing to operate the printing machine when needed. Shortly after Graham had started to work in the office, he mentioned that he had taken a course on offset printing machines while at school. From that day on, Graham was the company printer.

Aubrey (Bob) Silk had come to W.J. Hughes and Sons "Corn Flower" Limited as shipper-receiver in 1952, just as the company was making the move from 148 Kenwood Avenue to 102 Tycos Drive. Bob, a very enthusiastic curler, was from the Shelburne area, and was well-known throughout the region.. Shortly after his wife Ellen passed away, he decided to retire. The position of shipper was now open and, although the work day of a shipper was longer than office work, Graham was eager to take on this new challenge. He was now responsible for receiving and checking incoming shipments, storage in the warehouse, scheduling of the items to be cut, and ensuring that there was ample stock on hand to fill customers' orders promptly. It was necessary to stock cut items in the shipping room bins as efficiently as possible, to save himself steps when filling orders to be shipped. Sometimes Graham helped packers to pack the orders. Finally, he supervised the routing and the shipping of the orders. In the event that a customer would pick up an order to take home, Graham was always ready with a joke and a few laughs, a style that made him extremely well-liked by both customers and fellow employees. In later years, Graham found time to go into the cutting shop where he learned to do some fine cutting on glass.

A New Approach to Sales

Sales of Corn Flower had been declining in the Eaton's chain of stores since the late 1960s. Bob and Pete spoke with the principal buyer of the glass and china department during the 1970 Atlantic City Glass and China Show. Aware of shrinking sales, he suggested a new approach which he referred to as "supplier control." This proposed program placed the selection of wares directly on the supplier, who, knowing the best-selling products, would identify the items the buyer should have in the stores in order to obtain the most sales. A dollar quota, determined by the store classification, would be set for each store being serviced by the supplier. Periodic calls would be made at the various stores, to ascertain what had been sold and what required replacement. The theory was a simple one and Pete and Bob decided to initiate the program themselves on a trial basis.

After calling on two stores in Toronto, it became obvious that an organized system was essential for the program to be successful. A ring binder was set up for each outlet, listing the Corn Flower items being carried. When they called on a store, the existing items were entered in the book, indicating what had been sold and what should be reordered. An order was written on an Eaton's purchase order form and left with the department manager. If items remained unsold, they were taken back and a credit note issued. In effect, this was putting stock in a store on a guaranteed sale basis. It took time before some of the department managers could believe that stock was being returned to the supplier and not affecting the overall sales figures of their department.

Sometimes problems could develop when orders were left for the department manager to process. In some stores the department manager could sign the order, in others it was the store manager who signed the orders. This often led to delays. After several meetings with the Eaton's head glass buyer, it was arranged that the orders would be brought to him for signature, bypassing the managers of individual stores.

Often Pete and Bob would find all or part of the last order shipped still in the stock room on shelves, or sometimes not even unpacked. Before they could start to count the store stock, they would unpack, price and place the glass on the department display shelves themselves; it was almost like having their own store. They ordered, restocked, returned their own merchandise, and sometimes assisted customers. The two men serviced the Eaton's stores in southern Ontario.[17] When Bob retired, Pete continued on his own,

Originally, it had been hoped that once the complexities of the program had been worked out, it would be extended to the salesmen in the territories of the Maritime Provinces, the Ottawa and Montreal area and the Western Provinces. This was not possible, as the territories were too large for the CORN FLOWER salesmen to make the frequent calls required to maintain this approach.

Expanding Business in Hungary

IN 1970, THE BUSINESS WITH FERUNION OF HUNGARY GREW WHEN one of their glass factories was converted to the production of cut 24% lead crystal stemware. Ten different shapes and patterns were offered to CORN FLOWER for exclusive distribution in Canada. Initially, samples were shown to employees and families for a survey of first preferences. Seven lines were finally chosen, after declining three of the lines as being too similar to the others. Names for the different lines were selected and, as with CORN FLOWER, labels were made for each line to be

This *Canadian Jeweller* magazine advertisement of 1972 displays the seven lines of 24% lead crystal bearing the patterns cut in Hungary. Each had a W.J. Hughes sticker. They will become sought after by CORN FLOWER collectors who are beginning to add CORN FLOWER lines to their collections.

placed on every piece.[18] Each line had its own foil label with its individual name, identifying that it was "Imported Lead Crystal by W.J. Hughes 'Corn Flower'." The lines were available in goblet, sherbet, claret, sherry and liqueur glasses.

That same year, 1970, a soda lime glass stemware line was imported from Hungary. The Hughes Company named it "Cariad." It was a plain expensive-looking thin glass line that was priced for hotel or restaurant use, and became an profitable item for gift shops as well.

The following, listed in the 1971 National List of Advertisers, shows the diversity of products carried, besides CORN FLOWER, that the company had added since the death of W.J. Hughes in 1951, twenty years before:

Hughes & Sons Corn Flower Ltd., W.J.
102 Tycos Drive, Toronto
416-787-1135

Corn Flower Cut Glass Tableware
"Caramia"

Agents For: Fenton Milk Glass
　　　　　　 Viking "Epic"
　　　　　　 Imperial – Carnival Glass
　　　　　　 Rainbow Art Glass
　　　　　　 Country Store Candles & Flower Rings
　　　　　　 Holiday Import – Silver Replica Tableware
　　　　　　 Berry Pink Industries – Marbles

Sand-Blast & Machine Cut Tumblers
Full Lead Crystal Stemware
Corn Flower Aluminum Trays
Spanish Ceramic Figurines
Italian, Murano Glass, Figurines
Gift Boxed – Gold Decorated Tumbler Sets
"Anniversary" – Tumbler Sets – Aluminum Trays, etc.[19]

Looking For New Lines

Phillip "Pete" Kayser in 1975. The son-in-law of W.J. Hughes, he operated the company from 1951 to 1988.

I N 1971, LOIS, PETE AND BOB WERE IN THE ANNUAL ATLANTIC CITY China and Glass Show, looking for new items and prepared to service any Canadian buyers for the companies they represented. Usually pre-arranged times for meeting with customers were set up in advance, but in a show of this size connections were often incidental, especially to the party doing the buying. During periods not committed to meetings, they looked for new items through the isles of displays. One of them saw an impressive display of glassware with an adornment of candles and flower rings. It belonged to one of their glass suppliers who readily told them the source, Country Store Products. With thoughts of doing something similar in their Toronto Gift Show display, they placed a small order.

When they set up their own display in February, the candles and flower rings were used to enhance the look of the Fenton Milk Glass and the Viking coloured pieces. When the show opened and customers saw how attractive the glass looked with the candles and flower rings, most buyers wanted to buy the complete unit. Not wanting to lose potential sales, Pete immediately ordered more stock that very first morning.

Immediately following the show, Pete contacted the owners of Country Store Products. An agreement was reached which gave W.J. Hughes and Sons "Corn Flower"

Limited exclusive distribution for the items of Country Store Products across all of Canada. The candles and flower rings were volume sale items. Combining them with the Milk glass and coloured pieces gave a great surge to the sales of the glassware, until the world shortage of oil in 1975 brought an end to the manufacture of both candles and flower rings.

The year 1971 brought another new line to the CORN FLOWER company in the form of "Holiday Silverplate," a line of replicas of antique silver from England. These had an antimony base, and were silver-plated and lacquer-coated for tarnish resistance. Gerity Metal Products in Ohio manufactured them. The line consisted of a variety of table items including sugar and creamer set, salt and pepper set, compotes, bonbons, candle holders and serving dishes. Each piece had a label attached which read:

HOLIDAY
TARNISH PROTECTED
SILVER PLATE
Do not Polish – cleaning with
Damp cloth will retain luster
Distributed exclusively in Canada by
W.J. HUGHES & SONS, TORONTO
'Corn Flower' Limited

In 1982, the Imperial Glass by Lennox ceased production. The selection of Candlewick items had been lessening through the latter years. Near the end, orders would be accepted in turn lot quantities only; the last ordered by CORN FLOWER was for the 400/96 salt and pepper set, Lennox computer number 14460, CORN FLOWER number 29/2. The loss of Candlewick blanks was a sad blow to CORN FLOWER.

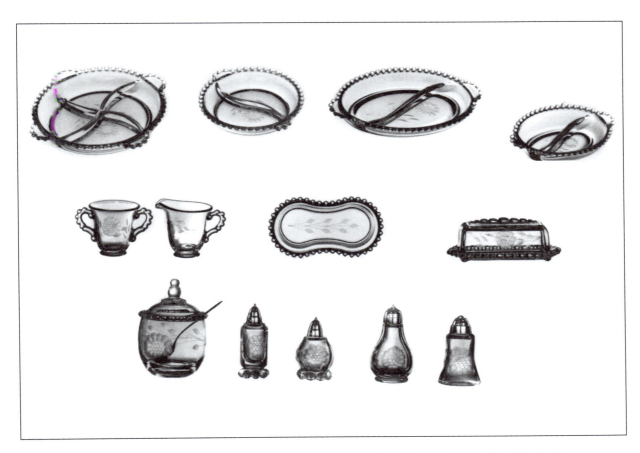

This page of the last catalogue produced in 1981 shows the only Imperial Candlewick blanks being cut and sold with W.J. Hughes "Corn Flower" at that time.

The Eighties

For the previous several years, the only Viking coloured glass that had been sold in Canada was their ruby glass, considered by many to be the finest on the market. The selection of clear blanks being sold by Corn Flower was limited to only a few pieces of the #42 line.

In 1984, the Fenton Art Glass Company, now being run by the sons of the previous management of Frank and Wilbur (Bill) Fenton, decided to open the Canadian market to another agent. They advised Pete of their intent, but he knew that the market tastes for Milk and coloured glass had sharply declined in the past years. He suggested that they would probably receive better representation from the other agent if he were to have their line exclusively for the territory. They agreed and Pete disposed of the Fenton stock at largely discounted prices in the next two gift shows.

The last sales of the Ferunion Lead Crystal lines were made in 1984. Factory prices had increased to a level that the goblets of the "Janessa" and the "Venora" lines had to retail at $70.00 each stem, more than the market would bear.

The Federal Glass Company of Columbus, Ohio, was owned by the Federal Box Company and as making boxes brought in more revenue, the parent company decided to close the less profitable operation. When the "last order" call was sent out to customers, Pete ordered two trailer loads of tumblers, the last items to be cut in the cutting shop.

As a result of these closings, Corn Flower was dependent on mouth blown glassware, except for a few items from the Indiana Glass Company and the Federal heavy base sham tumblers. Some of the glassware made

The last catalogue (1981) shows examples of American glass blanks.

in the mouth blown factories of the United States were still being ordered, however, the prices had escalated to the point that retail sales were minimal. While the Mid-Atlantic Glass Company of Ellenboro, West Virginia had the most reasonable costs, the factory was only producing glass a few days in a month because of lack of orders.

The decrease in availability of blanks for cutting, now that both Imperial and Viking were winding down operations, negated the purpose for the printing of new catalogues. The best that could be done was a consolidation of the mouth blown tableware that was available.

The lack of hand pressed glassware foretold the approaching end of one of the best known cut glass tableware firms in Canada. The CORN FLOWER design was still popular, but without quality blanks to cut, there was very little to sell, other than the mouth blown ware that was being produced and cut in Hungary.

In 1985, the factory at 102 Tycos Drive was sold. By then, less than one half of the factory was being used. The sandblasting cabinets and dust collectors had been sold. With the many feet of conveyor track not being used, the track was sold. For some time, a section of the warehouse was being rented out. The storage trailers that could not be sold were advertised in the newspaper as "Free for the Taking." They were all gone in a few days.

Paul McWilliams had started in the office with CORN FLOWER in his early twenties, in what he thought would be a short fill-in job. He and Pete were the only ones in the office thirty years later. Graham Kayser was the only one in the shipping-warehouse area. He had worked at Corn Flower for eighteen years. One cutter was left, cutting the Federal heavy base sham tumblers that had been the mainstay of their tumbler line since WWII.

Lois and Pete's son, Chris, had worked around the plant during school vacations, and became involved in packing, cutting tumblers and inspecting. He recalls the job:

> "There was a feeling of importance attached to doing this job, because I knew that once the glass passed my hands and got the W.J. Hughes "Cornflower" sticker applied to it as a quality piece, that glass was headed for someone's table somewhere. I truly felt a sense of pride and responsibility doing that job - after all, my father's reputation was on the line. If it was his reputation, it was mine as well. My father taught me the meaning of working hard and doing an honest day's work. He made it clear from the beginning that nothing would ever come easily unless you worked hard ... I watched him at work in his office. He was always a heads-down kind of man, who was at the office to get a job done, not to fool around. He did not object to jokes and laughter amongst the employees, as long as the work was getting done. He ran a tight ship and the product's quality is testament to his work ethic."[20]

Right up to closing, W.J. Hughes and Sons "Corn Flower" Limited remained a true "family" business.

In 1985, the Company leased a unit in a newly built industrial complex at 15 Connie Crescent in the Langstaff area of Concord, just north of Toronto. Six cutting frames were set up for cutting tumblers and a grinding machine and a polishing machine for making repairs to glass. At the front were a walk-in general office and a small private office. Between the front office and the cutting frames was the area for storage and shipping.

The company customer accounts list for 1987, 75 years after CORN FLOWER glassware was first sold, shows retail outlets as follows: British Columbia 5, Alberta 44, Saskatchewan 22, Manitoba 4, Ontario 286, Quebec 1, New Brunswick 17, Nova Scotia 20, Prince Edward Island 5, Newfoundland 1. Forty Eaton's stores and 37 Peoples Jewellers Limited across Canada carried the designed glassware.

By the end of January 1988, the inventory was finished. All but one cutting frame was gone for scrap metal. That cutting frame is now in the Dufferin County Museum & Archives, donated in October 2000 by Lois and Pete Kayser. The office was moved to Bobcaygeon, Ontario.

Although no longer producing CORN FLOWER, W.J. Hughes and Sons "Corn Flower" Limited still exists as a company today. The Company holds trademarks and patents and has financial investments. All company shares are held by a Holding Company whose shares, in turn, are held by Lois and Pete Kayser.

In 2000, Lucile Kennedy, the merchandise manager of Imperial Glass Corporation, USA remembers the company in a letter:

> "W.J. Hughes & Sons was a very important customer – not just because they were 'large volume' customers, but because they were understanding of the complexities of a hand-made glass factory versus a machine made glass factory. At one time, W.J. Hughes were also our 'Canadian Sales Force.'
>
> The personality of the people at W.J. Hughes helped to make our relationship very special. They were always pleasant and never asked for more than we would be able to give. They appreciated the special skills of our Imperial Glass artisans and we both remember the time that we shipped a full carload of Candlewick to them! Their Corn Flower cutting on Candlewick was extremely popular and today it is highly prized by Collectors in the States and in Canada.

I never had the privilege of meeting Mr. Hughes but I enjoyed my association with Lois and Pete Kayser and Bob Prouse. As you can guess, I have many fine memories of the folks at W.J. Hughes."[21]

Today, people from many walks of life collect CORN FLOWER. It has become a recognized Canadian product that remains in demand by both Canadian and American collectors. The coloured glass is the most difficult to find, but some collectors are slowly putting sets together as young brides did decades ago. Fortunately, the beautiful design cut on Candlewick has added thousands upon thousands of pieces that collectors can look for in the many antique and market outlets. Both the treasured pieces that are handed down as family heirlooms and the continually increasing number of avid collectors are a wonderful tribute to a young man raised in poverty and in a motherless family by a dedicated father, in a small rural village in Dufferin County. William John "Jack" Hughes was and remains creatively Canadian.

EPILOGUE

The Future of Corn Flower

Corn Flower today is part of Canadian manufacturing history. It is collected and cherished by many Canadians from coast to coast. But what of the future? Will subsequent generations of our country know the name W.J. Hughes and Sons "Corn Flower" Ltd. and recognize the pattern so delicately cut in a piece of clear or coloured glass?

The future of Corn Flower lies in the Dufferin County Museum & Archives where the corporate and family memory of W.J. Hughes and the pattern Corn Flower are now being protected by the facility. It is a rare opportunity that allows museum staff to work directly with the people involved with a historic business or event, such as has been possible with Pete and Lois Kayser. Pete spent countless weeks making sure that the story written in this book was as accurate as possible. They have been generous with their knowledge, their memories and their Corn Flower possessions which they have donated to the DCMA. The remaining items of historical interest regarding the Corn Flower business which they had kept are protected and housed in a climate and light-controlled environment in the very community where their father was raised. The policy of the museum clearly states that this material will never be dispersed or sold. Although some of the original material is not available to the public for conservation reasons, all of these archival materials and photographs have been carefully copied and may be consulted by collectors and researchers. It is hoped that Hughes family "collections" still exist and will be donated to the museum.

The Dufferin County Museum & Archives actively collects CORN FLOWER glass and other product lines sold by the company. This collection is also available to the public to study and enjoy. Those who are already CORN FLOWER collectors can learn more about what they have acquired. New enthusiasts, drawn to the glass when they see it for the first time in the museum display cases, may later purchase their first piece in an antique show or find a set of stemware in an aunt's or grandmother's cabinet. Several important collections and single treasured family pieces have been donated to the museum to honour the memory of a loved one or by generous collectors who wish to see their collections remain intact and enjoyed by the public.

The future of CORN FLOWER is found at the annual Corn Flower Festival held at the Dufferin County Museum & Archives on the weekend closest to June 11th, the birthday of Lois (Hughes) Kayser. The first festival was held in 1999 with a few invited guests and in three years has grown into an event that attracts hundreds of collectors, eager for new information on Jack Hughes and the different blanks used by him. Collectors are encouraged to bring pieces for

Pete and Lois Kayser, 1991. W.J. Hughes' son-in-law and daughter still own the company, W.J. Hughes "Corn Flower" Limited.

The Dufferin County Museum and Archives staff work with Pete Kayser to reassemble the restored "cutting" machine used for cutting CORN FLOWER circa 1960 to 1988. Left to right: Steve Brown, Archivist; Pete Kayser, owner of W.J. Hughes "Corn Flower" Limited; Darrell Keenie, General Manager; and Wayne Townsend, Curator.

Corn Flower family reminiscences inside the restored Historic Corbetton Methodist Church Building on the grounds of the DCMA. On the stage, Lois (Hughes) Kayser, her husband Pete Kayser, and cousin Don Hughes, whose father was a Dufferin businessman, share their memories of the Hughes family and of the company's growth from a one-man operation into a recognized household name.

identification by Lois and Pete Kayser and to show them off to the other guests. In 2000, the event was used to feature the showing of a 40mm film, about four minutes in length, showing W.J. Hughes cutting his Corn Flower pattern on a ten-inch Imperial Candlewick plate. This footage was filmed in 1948. This event will continue at the museum annually, with the focus each year on new information from collectors. Also it is hoped that the event will extend the data base of Corn Flower blanks kept at the museum by having undiscovered authenticated pieces photographed during the Festival. The occasion also ensures that the extensive Corn Flower collection will be available for the public to view at least once a year, and not forgotten on the museum shelves. More and more descendants of the many Hughes families are attracted to the event where they enjoy sharing family information. Sometimes they are meeting each other for the first time, and then plan to annually renew these friendships.

The future of Corn Flower lies with the many Canadian families who pass down the treasured pieces of glassware from generation to generation. For many, a little more knowledge about the glass tableware that came from their parents' and grandparents' cupboards will bring that family member's memory closer to the heart each time the piece is enjoyed by the next generation.

The future of Corn Flower is found in the collectors. These are the people who get up before the crack of dawn to go over the tables at an outdoor antique show or sit patiently for hours waiting for that single beautiful piece of Corn Flower at an auction sale. The collector is the individual who drives friends crazy by enthusiastically repeating the number of Corn Flower pieces collected to date for the hundredth time. The future is also with the gracious host who serves a snack to a guest on a favourite Candlewick plate.

The future of Corn Flower lies along the

The Corn Flower "Roadshow" at the Corn Flower Festival. Visitors bring their Corn Flower heirlooms to the Dufferin County Museum & Archives to be identified and authenticated by Lois and Pete Kayser, former operators of W.J. Hughes & Sons "Corn Flower" Limited, and Walter Lemiski (centre), President of the Canadian Depression Glass Association.

back roads of rural Dufferin County. Along the way you will still see remnants of the way life was in 1881 when Jack Hughes was born. While some of the buildings are in disrepair, others are carefully restored to their original historic beauty by a new generation of settlers coming to the area, fleeing the busy city life. The little creek still runs by Bowling Green where the small Methodist cemetery still exists. The Grand River still runs through Riverview, the picturesque beginning of that Heritage River, past the buildings that once housed the general store and the school. There are still many relatives of Jack and Hazel (Graham) Hughes living in the Dufferin area, such people as Krista Taylor of East Garafraxa, Beth Cleave of Amaranth, Mildred Taylor of Grand Valley, Bonnie White of Orangeville and Murray McLeod of Caledon. The families and friends of Mike Gray, George Scace and Aubrey Silk recall stories told of the glass shop with low ceilings in the basement of a house at 212 Wychwood Avenue where these men once worked.

Tales of a wonderful generous relative named Jack arriving for a visit with the gift of a piece of glass on which he had cut a beautiful floral design are still fondly remembered. These grandchildren and great grandchildren still live along these same back roads where W.J. Hughes grew up and where he developed his desire to succeed. Perhaps along this road somewhere today is someone's son or daughter who will make a contribution to Canadian history as did Jack Hughes so many years ago. This potential is the future of this and every community.

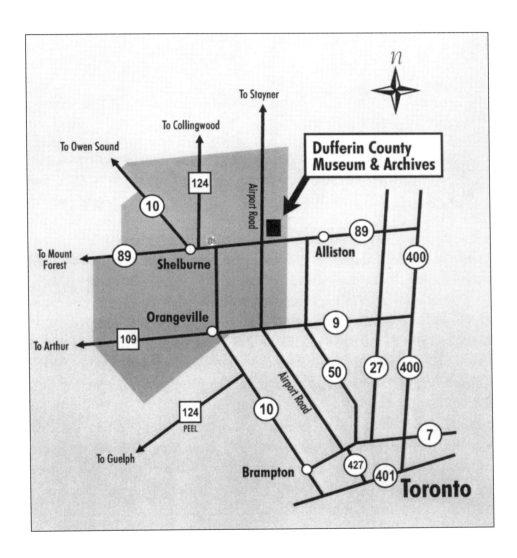

Map showing the locations of the Dufferin County Museum and Archives. The shaded area defines Dufferin County, birthplace of W.J. Hughes.

APPENDIX I

Corn Flower Blanks: 1914 to 1944

North American glass manufacturing underwent major changes between the two World Wars. During the first decade that W.J. Hughes began acquiring glass blanks on which he cut his Corn Flower (1914-1924), American glass producers were essentially manufacturing what collectors today refer to as "crystal" glass. In Depression Glass collectors' lingo, this simply means clear uncoloured glass and does not refer to lead crystal. It must be noted that there were no Canadian glass companies who produced the quality of glass that Hughes was seeking.

Starting in the mid-1920s, besides mass-production of glassware impacting the marketplace, coloured glassware began to emerge as an important new element. With the diminishing costs of production, thanks to new technologies, glass companies could afford the little bit extra required to colour the glassware. Company after company quickly jumped on this colour bandwagon. The basic range of colours were transparent amber, pink, green and yellow, although the spectrum of glass colours was widened with various shades of these basics and through experimentation with opaque glass. The September 1929 issue of the influential homemaker's magazine *Better Homes and Gardens* included an article entitled "Serve It in Colored Glassware." The author declared that: "The aristocracy of colored glassware is in its richness and warmness, and the former preponderance of the frigid and sheer-crystal glassware on our table wholly lacked this. Whatever it is, serve it in glass!"[1]

Although one tends to think automatically of Depression era glassware in terms of its distinctive colours, one must keep in mind that crystal never was totally out of the picture. From the teens through to the mid-1920s Hughes would have been working on only crystal blanks. From the mid-1920s up to the early 1940s colours were available and utilized for CORN FLOWER. However, large quantities of the tried and true traditional crystal wares were still being produced throughout the 1930s. By the mid-1940s, fashion had shifted once again, and colour was virtually gone from the marketplace. Besides a very small number of ruby-footed and handled items from the mid-1940s, one can categorically state that any coloured glassware cut with CORN FLOWER must have been produced between 1925 and 1945. The greatest run of coloured CORN FLOWER is actually a narrower period encompassing the 1930s.

What was essential for Hughes, first and foremost, was quality of glass. The mass-produced glasswares, what is commonly referred to today as Depression Glass, used glass that was scarcely better than bottle glass. Huge tanks of glass were fed into machinery that produced massive quantities of glassware, the whole process involving very little quality control and virtually no hand finishing. Inherent in such low-grade glass were bubbles, lack of clarity and non-uniformity of shape. To cover such deficiencies, many Depression Glass lines were molded in patterns that covered much of the glass surface, thus disguising the deficiencies. During the same era, a second type of glass was being produced known today as Elegant Glassware.

Elegant production, also called hand glass, was made in considerably smaller batches with a better quality of raw materials (the glass metal). During production this glassware often underwent further stages with more finishing or decorating done by teams of skilled glass craftsmen and women. Gold trims, ground bases, cuttings, plate etchings and fire polishing were among the extra measures taken with this finer quality product. Hughes required blanks that were not only of superior quality, but which were uncluttered in design and left large clear surfaces on which to better showcase his original CORN FLOWER design.

All the companies that Hughes ordered glass from were situated in the tri-state area of Pennsylvania, Ohio and West Virginia. These three states alone were home to all the major American glass producers and accounted for over ninety percent of glass production in North America throughout this entire period. To give some notion of the scope of glass production in this era, we only have to look at West Virginia in the late 1930s. Given years of down-sizing, amalgamations and the Depression, there were still over one hundred and fifty glass factories in 1938 in West Virginia alone. Of course, this number includes pressed tableware producers and elegant glass factories, as well as mills manufacturing everything from bottles to windshields. Add decorating shops to this number and the number of people involved in the glass industry is seen to be very substantial indeed.

A total of eight companies have been identified to date as suppliers of blanks for Hughes "Corn Flower" during the first thirty years. This number may be somewhat confounded by reports that Hughes would undertake custom cuttings for customers who brought in their own uncut pieces for treatment. These eight companies were all major players in the American elegant glass field: Fostoria, Heisey, Imperial, Lancaster, New Martinsville, Paden City, Tiffin Glass, and West Virginia Specialty Glass.

W.J. Hughes imported almost exclusively American elegant glassware blanks for production of his Corn Flower over the first thirty years of business. To this date, little documentation has been unearthed from these early years. Hughes apparently believed that word-of-mouth was the best way to "grow" a business. Consequently, and unfortunately for researchers, he did virtually nothing to advertise his wares through standard trade magazines or through print media. There are, however, several 1920s Heisey invoices mentioned in Hughes "Corn Flower" correspondence from the late 1960s. Some additional evidence has been gathered through the viewing of Corn Flower collections and observing what has been available at Depression Glass Shows, general line shows and antique markets. But, by far the most informative, intriguing and, at the same time, puzzling source of information about glass blanks purchased by W.J. Hughes in the 1930s is found in the advertising photographs. This "catalogue" was produced by the Toronto-based photographer, J. Thornley Wrench, in the late 1930s for use in the Hughes' showroom and for his first distributor, Haddy, Body and Company.

The very first photograph of this early catalogue begins with

Top Row:
Fostoria #2375
Sweetmeat; Lemon
Dish; Whip Cream

Bottom Row:
New Martinsville 5″
Nut Dish; Fostoria
2500 4-part 8″ Sunray
Relish

frustration. Any one of at least a half dozen different firms could have produced these round plates. The same conundrum emerges on the pages where the stemware is illustrated. However, with much of the early stemware it is difficult if not impossible to definitively identify the maker, since very similar shapes were made by a number of different firms and are simply "too generic a shape" to perhaps ever conclusively establish origins.

What is made clear from the 1930s "photograph/catalogue" is that several Fostoria items were definitely cut with CORN FLOWER. Pictured on the top row of one photograph is a sweetmeat, lemon dish and whip cream bowl. All show the distinctive Fostoria bow-type handles. This blank, #2375, was used by Fostoria for two of its most popular plate etchings, the exquisite June and Versailles patterns. Colours in production were azure (blue), crystal, green, rose (pink) and topaz/gold tint. Hand written notes on the edge of this catalogue page seem to indicate that these items were ordered by Hughes in all the above colours with the exception of azure. Pictured on the same page is a 4-part relish in

APPENDIX I 219

Fostoria's line #2510, Sunray (1935-1943). Notations on this linen-back page lead one to believe that twenty-four dozen of the Sunray items were ordered in crystal.

The Fostoria Glass Company began in Fostoria, Ohio in 1887. There they remained until the source of cheap natural gas that enticed them there began to run low whereupon they relocated to Moundsville, West Virginia in 1891. They started out producing oil lamps, pressed glass for home and hotel, vases, and candelabra. By the early 1900s, Fostoria changed focus to glass for the household — from stemware to tableware, to occasional pieces. They introduced their durable cubist American pattern as well as many more refined lines with a large variety of etchings. By the 1920s, they ranked as one of the foremost of the hand-glass producers. In 1924, Fostoria first introduced colours and, by 1926, they brought out the first complete glass dinner services. Various of Fostoria's lines appeared in no fewer than a dozen different colours, as well as in crystal. One colour for which they were noted was Topaz, a golden yellow shade. They had a chemical research laboratory and a special design department replete with top artists. Such was the quality of their products that naturally their glassware was priced accordingly. This is perhaps the reason that not a lot of Fostoria is to be found cut with Hughes "CORN FLOWER" — the price was simply prohibitive. Hughes was aiming his marketing at the middle-class consumer. The Fostoria fires were finally cooled in 1986 after nearly a century of extraordinary production.

The next advertising photograph yields up items from another one of the very large players in the elegant glass field, the Heisey Glass Company. Pictured are two items from the distinctive and well-designed Fern line #1495, produced from 1937-1941. The uncluttered surfaces of this pattern obviously provided an excellent working area for the CORN FLOWER cut. Another elegant, cleanly designed line imported from Heisey was the Empress #1401 line, produced between 1930-1938. Celery trays in Heisey's Sahara (yellow), one of their top-selling colours are found with the Hughes "CORN FLOWER" bud. The bud cut was utilized due to the narrow panels available on the tray surfaces.

Augustus H. Heisey opened his glass factory in Newark, Ohio in 1896. Through its half a century of production, Heisey Glass became

Assortment of items including New Martinsville Radiance and Heisey Fern Pattern

synonymous with quality glassware. Heisey's renown arose from the purity and consistency of basic materials. A fair number, but not all, of Heisey items are signed with their trademark "H" in a diamond.

The sole evidence of pre-war invoices of glass purchased from any company by W.J. Hughes comes from secondary sources. Early in 1969, Pete Kayser and Robert Prouse of Hughes "Corn Flower" corresponded with Lucile J. Kennedy, assistant to the President of the Imperial Glass Corporation, and with the Heisey researcher Clarence W. Vogel. Vogel was in the midst of writing his four volumes on Heisey glassware. The letters mention invoices dating from the late 1920s. From these notes we learn more about the scope of blanks utilized, however there is no information about the size of the orders. The only indication of the colour of these items was for the #113 Mars candlestick that was labelled

"Flamingo" — the Heisey term for pink, their top selling colour produced between 1925 and 1935. We suspect that some of these items may also have been ordered in crystal, Moongleam (green) or in Sahara (yellow).

ITEM NUMBER	LINE NAME	DATES	ITEM DESCRIPTION	INVOICE DATE
112	Mercury	1926-1957	Candlestick 3″	23 Sept. 1926
113	Mars	1926-1933	Candlestick 3″	23 Sept. 1926
1023	Yeoman	1922-1937	Creamer and covered sugar	25 May 1926
1183	Revere	1913-1935	Jelly, 5½″, 2 handled	
1185	Yeoman	1922-1937	Celery Tray, 12″	
1186	Yeoman	1913-1957	Cup and saucer	
1229	Octagon	1925-1937	Cheese Dish, 6″, 2 handled	
1229	Octagon	1925-1937	Mint, 6″, 2 handled	
1229	Octagon	1925-1937	Muffin Plate, 10″, 2 handled	
1229	Octagon	1925-1937	Muffin Plate, 12″, 2 handled	22 Oct. 1926
1229	Octagon	1925-1937	Sandwich plate, 10″, 2 handled	
1229	Octagon	1925-1937	Sandwich plate, 12″, 2 handled	22 Oct. 1926
3350	Wabash	1922-1939	Comport and cover, footed, 6″	23 Sept. 1926
4163	Whaley	1919-1953	Tankard, 54oz	

It would certainly appear that the Heisey Glass Company was a large supplier for Hughes "Corn Flower" through the earlier years. After having been at the forefront of the glass industry for some sixty years, the Heisey factory closed in 1956, at which time the Imperial Glass Company purchased the moulds.

Although not represented in the Hughes 1930s advertising photographs, Imperial Candlewick cut with CORN FLOWER would emerge at the end of the company's third decade as the most enduring of their lines. By the mid-1950s Hughes "Corn Flower" listed over one hundred Candlewick items in their sales catalogue produced from 1953 to 1956. The Imperial Glass Company began its long existence at Bellaire, Ohio in 1904. Producing glass until 1984, Imperial was one of America's premiere hand-glass (elegant glass) producers. It appears that Hughes' long association with the Imperial Glass Company began in the late 1930s. Candlewick, Imperial's 400 line, one of the most recognized and longest running elegant glass patterns ever produced, was for some four

Top Row:
Lancaster #879
cream/sugar; Tiffin #6
cream/sugar

Bottom Row:
Tiffin #14185
cream/sugar; Tiffin #3
cream/sugar

decades a mainstay of the Hughes Company catalogues. According to glass researcher, Willard Kolb, company president Earl W. Newton brought back to the Imperial Company from New York an item in the "French Cannon Ball" pattern in 1933. Similar patterns such as the United States Glass company's "Atlas" line and the McKee Glass Company's "Rays" may also have helped inspire Candlewick designers. After a couple of years of experimentation, Imperial craftsmen developed a uniquely designed block mould that did not show the joint marks on the items. The signs of mould marks on the distinctive beads were easily removed during the warming-in process. What resulted was a clean, clear, uncluttered surface perfect for cuttings. By 1936, Candlewick was being promoted and, by the late 1930s, many new items were being added to the growing Candlewick catalogue. By the mid-1940s some two hundred and fifty different Candlewick items were available from which Hughes could choose. For the most part the uncluttered, smooth surfaces were ideal for the light cutting or gray cutting of CORN FLOWER. A large number of

Top Row:
Lancaster #869/8
10¼" Bowl; 1377/3 7"
Candy; T767/3 9"
crimped Bowl

Bottom Row:
Lancaster Bowl and
T1831/6 6" Rose Bowl
and unattributed
Decanter and
Whiskey

items were never cut on due to rounded surfaces, small cutting areas, awkwardness of cutting on certain items or because of prohibitive costs. On some of the smaller items, such as 400/172, the 4½" Mint Heart, the full flower could not be accommodated so a star pattern was cut instead. Their relationship was long and fruitful, with Hughes "Corn Flower" in later years becoming the sole agent for Imperial Glass in Canada.

A half dozen items manufactured by the Lancaster Glass Company appear in the early Hughes catalogue. One advertising photograph features a cream and sugar set, Lancaster No. 879, shown as the left pair on the top row, while the other pictures a quintet of bowls. The Lancaster colours of interest to CORN FLOWER include green produced from 1925, deep pink introduced in 1926, and topaz (the trade name for yellow) made from 1930. Items such as the centre handled sandwich tray, Lancaster No.88, appeared in 1923 and were specifically intended for firms like Hughes, as the ads stated they would be ideal for "light cutters and decorators."[2] The CORN FLOWER that one primarily finds on Lancaster blanks are items in topaz, with only a little green and deep pink being found. Most Lancaster blanks cut with CORN FLOWER are distinctive with their pointed edges, ornate handles and scroll feet. Item number T899/4, a centre-handled sandwich tray (see Plate 24) illustrates two of these characteristic Lancaster stylistic features, as do the items shown in adjacent photographs featuring Lancaster pieces. Candy dishes, rose bowls, centre-handled sandwich trays, two-handled cake plates, candlesticks and stemware are amongst items that were utilized by Hughes.

The Lancaster Glass Company set up shop in 1908 in Lancaster, Ohio. The firm was run by two brothers, Lucien and Philip Martin who had worked with the Hocking Glass Company. By 1924, Lancaster was controlled by the large Hocking company. Besides tableware, Lancaster produced a large array of occasional items such as bonbons, bowls and vases. Their in-house work on decorating their own blanks puts them in the category of elegant glass houses. However, their quality of glass was on the lower rungs of the elegant lineage. While in many respects the quality was quite good, it certainly not up to the high standard of the Fostoria or Heisey Glass Companies. Although the factory remained in use for many more decades after, the Lancaster name was in use only until 1937. From that date on the parent company, the Hocking Glass Company, began to market all their subsidiary's products under the Hocking banner.

There are two quite outstanding lines of New Martinsville Company glassware that appear in the early Hughes "Corn Flower" catalogue. At the end of 1932 the company released its No.37 line, better known as Moondrops. The pattern featured a raised circle on the bottom sections of the blanks "reminiscent of the age of chivalry." It grew to be a large line with over seventy different pieces being made. In the "photograph/catalogue" a Moondrops cocktail shaker with CORN FLOWER cut is pictured. Essentially, it is a large mug topped off with a metal lid. Matching stemware and a cream and sugar set are found in the same photo. The Dufferin County Museum collection contains this shaker in both amber and in green. An ad from 1934, from *Pottery, Glass and Brass Salesman* lists the cocktail set as "The Butler's Delight."[3] The other major pattern for CORN FLOWER was line No.42, Radiance.

Unveiled in 1936, Radiance, called "Tear Drop" by the Hughes, became one of their favourite blanks used over many years. New Martinsville's introductory ad stated that "while each piece is highly decorative in itself it is so designed as to allow ample space for decorations and cuttings."[4] Colours notated on the advertising photos indicate that the 11" plate was purchased in crystal, amber and blue, while the two-part 8" relish colours were crystal, amber, blue, rose, and green. Viking Glass Company carried on producing Radiance, primarily in crystal, after taking over the company in 1944. The line was quite an extensive one, numbering some forty pieces. Items frequently seen include various bowls, the butter dish, relishes, plates, and cream/sugar sets on trays.

Beginning in the 1930s, New Martinsville became one of the larger suppliers of glassware to Hughes. At their opening in 1900, the New Martinsville plant began to manufacture tableware, lamps and novelties. In the glass industry trade paper, *American Flint*, from 1923 it was reported that New Martinsville was employing "eleven cutters working

Items attributed to New Martinsville
Top Row:
3-footed Bowl;
Table Tumbler;
"Moondrops" Cream and Sugar

Bottom Row:
3-footed Bowl;
"Moondrops" 4 oz Tumbler and Cocktail Shaker; Mayo Set

Top Row:
New Martinsville 2-part and 3-part Relishes

Bottom Row:
Radiance 11" Plate; 8½" Salad Plate; 6½" Sherbet Plate

full time and cannot keep up with the orders."[5] Aware of the needs of their own in-house cutters, the company was designing blanks with cutting in mind. Their own ads stated that "any style of cutting desired" could be supplied.

Also in the Dufferin County Museum's collection is the splendid New Martinsville's #103, three-part divided, covered candy. Originally unveiled as "Our New Candy Box De Luxe" in June of 1935, it was available from New Martinsville in "crystal, evergreen, Ritz Blue, amber and rose." Retail for this stylish item was 98 cents. The #103 candy dish as well as other New Martinsville items have been seen with a stretched variant of the CORN FLOWER design. These pieces may have been cut by a rival cutter or perhaps by a Hughes craftsman while on break time. New Martinsville was to remain an important supplier for Hughes "Corn Flower" under the Viking banner well after their closure in 1944.

The item illustrated in the next advertising photo, second from the left in the bottom row, is Paden City's 3-part Winged Relish, advertised in

1934 by Paden City. David Fisher, who had been a part of the New Martinsville Glass Company, established the glass plant in Paden City, West Virginia in 1916. Production was essentially of crystal pressed tablewares. Paden City grew to be known for its over two dozen colours that it developed through the 1920s. As with the other companies from which Hughes bought, Paden City was a hand glass or elegant glass factory that made fine-blown tumblers and stemware and had specialized decorating departments. Because of close proximity to New Martinsville and with workers switching back and forth between the firms, both firms products show many stylistic similarities. The Paden City Glass Manufacturing Company remained in business until 1951.

A wide range of Tiffin Glass Company blanks utilized by W.J. Hughes are illustrated on approximately one quarter of the pages of the his early catalogue. One photograph shows the range of footed tumblers and stems that Hughes imported. The two Tiffin lines pictured are the

Top Row:
Selection of Trays and Relishes attributed to Fostoria and Paden City Glass Companies

228 CORN FLOWER - CREATIVELY CANADIAN

#15020 footed tumblers and the #15024 stemware line. In this era, CORN FLOWER was typically cut on three sizes of footed tumblers: the smallest being the oyster cocktail or whiskey; the mid-size the seltzer; and the large size the table tumbler. A half dozen sizes of stems were regularly cut including cocktails, sundaes, saucer champagnes, wines, sherries and goblets. Names of similar items may be different within companies or even change through the years within one firm. Many of the Tiffin stemware lines are quite distinctive with their ornate stems. Other Tiffin items cut with CORN FLOWER include baskets, candy dishes, comports, handled cake plates, candlesticks, creamer/sugar sets, plates, relish dishes,

Bottom Row:
Tiffin #15024, 9 oz Goblet; 6 oz Saucer Champagne; Sundae; 3½ oz Cocktail

sundae dishes, trays, water pitchers and vases.

Although done alphabetically, it is somehow apt that one of the biggest supplier of glass blanks for CORN FLOWER is the one of the final companies that we look at in this study of the CORN FLOWER advertising photographs. All signs point to the Tiffin Glass Company as being one of the major pre-WWII providers of glass blanks for Hughes "Corn Flower." This is not surprising when one ascertains that during this period Tiffin produced as much, if not more than most of the other large glass firms.

Tiffin was actually one of an association of nineteen glass factories that joined forces in 1891 as the U.S. Glass Company. Previously, the company had been the A.J. Beatty and Sons Glass Company, of Steubenville, Ohio. They moved to Tiffin, Ohio in July of 1888, thanks to that town's generous enticement of five years of free natural gas, thirty-five thousand dollars and land worth fifteen thousand dollars. The amalgamation of so many glass firms gave U.S. Glass a distinct advantage. Through specialization, sheer size and use of non-union workers the conglomerate strove to swamp the competition. In 1923, U.S. Glass provided offerings of some "25,000 pieces to Choose From!" in its catalogues. In the beginning, Factory R, the Tiffin factory, specialized in producing hundreds of thousands of pressed glass tumblers per week along with barware. Gradually the plant began to focus more on blown wares.

Starting in 1914, Tiffin was switched to producing higher-quality blown and molded tablewares and stemware entirely. By 1927, the brain trust at the United States Glass Company decided it would be advantageous for marketing purposes for their products be known for their quality — the Tiffin quality. The Tiffin factory became the flagship of the organization. When the company sought to cash in on the Tiffin name, it created a separate label for Tiffin — TIFFIN superimposed over a large "T" within a shield on a gold paper label. Although the majority of Tiffin glass was produced in Ohio, some items were manufactured at Factory G, Glassport, Pennsylvania and at Factory K in Pittsburgh, Pennsylvania.

As with the other major glass producers, starting in the mid-1920s the Tiffin Glass Company created a large palette of glass colours. The marketing geniuses were not content to call their products simply pink, green or yellow, but rather had a delightful array of descriptors: Rose

Pink, Reflex Green, Sky Blue, Mandarin, Lilac, Twilite, Canary, Emerald Green, Amber, Ruby, Amethyst, Amberina, Royal Blue, Old Gold and Black The colours that tend to be seen most often are: Rose Pink, Reflex Green and Mandarin (amber). The stunning Royal blue and lilac, scarcer Tiffin colours, are found more infrequently. One quite remarkable colour of glass brought out by Tiffin was called Twilight. The chemistry of this colour allowed it to fluctuate between a purple shade and a blue shade depending on lighting conditions. Of course, many of the big elegant glass houses of that age produced similar recipes, such as Fostoria's Wisteria, Heisey's Alexandrite, and Cambridge's Heatherbloom. Various items including stemware and vases have been seen with the CORN FLOWER cut in this scarcer type of glass.

Tiffin continued to produce glass through until 1980, although the company had been purchased by a couple of new owners after the 1962 bankruptcy of the original firm. As is the case with other elegant glass companies, as costs rose after 1945 Hughes could not profitably continue to purchase from firms who had been his earlier major suppliers. Tiffin appears as one of the most important of the seven major players to sell to Hughes "Corn Flower" through the 1930s.

Although no items have been identified in the advertising photographs as West Virginia Specialty Glass items, blanks were acquired from them starting as early as 1939. Purchases from West Virginia Specialty are verified in some of the few existing business cheques from Hughes "Corn Flower." An order for $177.21 worth of merchandise was placed in 1939; an order for $44.55 was placed in 1941; and an order for $1368.97 was place in 1942. Unfortunately no invoices indicating what was items were bought exist.

Through the 1920s Louie Wohinc gradually expanded his glass empire in Weston, West Virginia. He was a former glass worker who rose to become the manager of the Weston Glass Company in 1919, and finally the owner of a number of glass factories. The West Virginia Glass Specialty Company was established when Wohinc took over the Crescent Window Glassworks in 1929. After retooling, the factory produced a variety of beverage wares such as water sets, punch sets, decanters and cocktail shaker sets, as well as console sets and vases. The photograph in Part II on page 83 featuring a water set, shows the easily recognized Louie

APPENDIX I   231

Wohinc style. Certainly, other firms like West Virginia Specialty which have been little documented may come to light in time as having been suppliers of glass blanks to W. J. Hughes in the early years. While this study of the first thirty years of Corn Flower production does not claim to be definitive by any means, what emerges is at least a good starting point for further inquiries.

Although both crystal and coloured Corn Flower glassware has long been collected and cherished by collectors, it is the early items that are the most prized. The added details that lower labour costs allowed, and the delightful palette of colours from the mid-1920s through to the 1940s, add a further dimension for Corn Flower lovers. With the establishment of an important Corn Flower collection and archives at the Dufferin County Museum we look forward to learning and understanding yet more about this early period of Hughes "Corn Flower" production. Pete and Lois Kayser have gone a long way in giving us the tools to finally understand much more about Corn Flower glass by donating treasured Corn Flower catalogues and family papers. We have now come to know what is authentic Corn Flower and to begin to realize even more fully the importance of the historical ties between Hughes "Corn Flower" and most of the major American hand glass manufacturers of the twentieth century. The longevity of this gorgeous glassware in itself serves as a tribute to the Hughes "Corn Flower" Company. Corn Flower is indeed a truly amazing Canadian success story!

Walter T. Lemiski, M.A.

APPENDIX II

Trademarks and "Copies" of Corn Flower

THE NAME CORN FLOWER, AS USED TO REFER TO "CUT GLASS tableware" was registered to W.J. Hughes, many years before he incorporated his business. He had used the name since 1914 in association with the cut glass products he produced. When the company of "W.J. Hughes & Sons "Corn Flower" Limited was formed in 1950, all registered trademarks in his name were transferred to the new company.

In the glassware and giftware trade, the trademark CORN FLOWER was registered to W.J. Hughes and Sons "Corn Flower" Limited, exclusively. The use of it verbally or otherwise, by any individual or organization, in reference to a product not from the Company, was an infringement of the use of the "Trademark." A product must have passed "through the hands" of the Company to qualify for the designation "Corn Flower." This stipulation was comparable to Ford's "Lincoln" and General Motor's "Cadillac." Thus, the well-known gold and blue CORN FLOWER label was a registered Trademark of the Company, which had the "proprietary" use of the label. This label had been applied to every piece of CORN FLOWER cut glassware since 1932, and was absolute proof that the item was CORN FLOWER. The advertising programs presented by Walsh Advertising Company, always stressed, "look for the blue and gold label."

Some associated products were made "exclusively" for, and according to specifications of the Company. New trademark registrations for "designs," and extensions of existing trademarks were obtained for aluminum trays, ovenware, mugs and tumblers.

Over time some copies of Corn Flower glassware appeared in the marketplace. R. G. Sherriff, an ex-employee, began his own business of cutting glass tableware. He cut a design he called "Cosmos," with a ribbed flower petal, but soon began cutting a "copy" of Corn Flower in his Adelaide Street (Toronto) place of business. A label was applied on his "copy" that was the same size, shape, colour and printing style as the registered Corn Flower label. In 1948, the Supreme Court of Ontario ordered the use of the "copy" label stopped. Throughout the years, a few other cutters have cut "copies" but none was significant. These were relatively short-lived. Any good glasscutter with ability and skill can cut a copy of any design, but the quality of the glass blank being cut is the determination of a superior or inferior product. Corn Flower blanks were always chosen with premium quality in mind. That standard of glass blank is difficult if not impossible to find today.

In 1959, Dr. Harold G. Fox QC, the patent and trademark lawyer for the Company, commissioned a survey of 75 retailers and 200 housewives regarding the name Corn Flower as it applies to houseware products. The instructions to the interviewers stated, "This survey is to be conducted among housewives and among dealers in cut glassware in Canadian cities and towns to find out if they are familiar with the words Corn Flower and especially to determine whether they know Corn Flower as a brand name or Trademark, and if it refers to just one company or many companies." The results indicated that the name of W.J. Hughes was synonymous with the name Corn Flower.

APPENDIX III

Family Tree

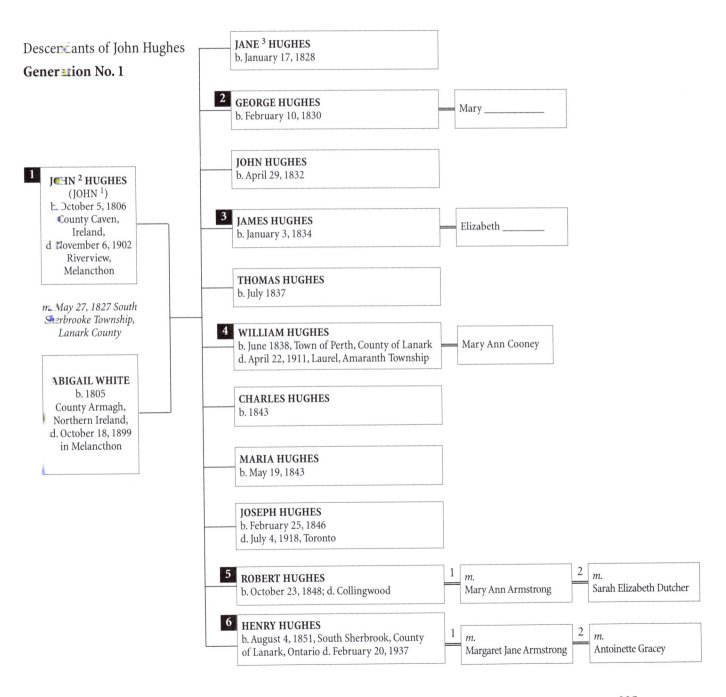

APPENDIX III 235

Descendants of John Hughes **Generation No. 2**

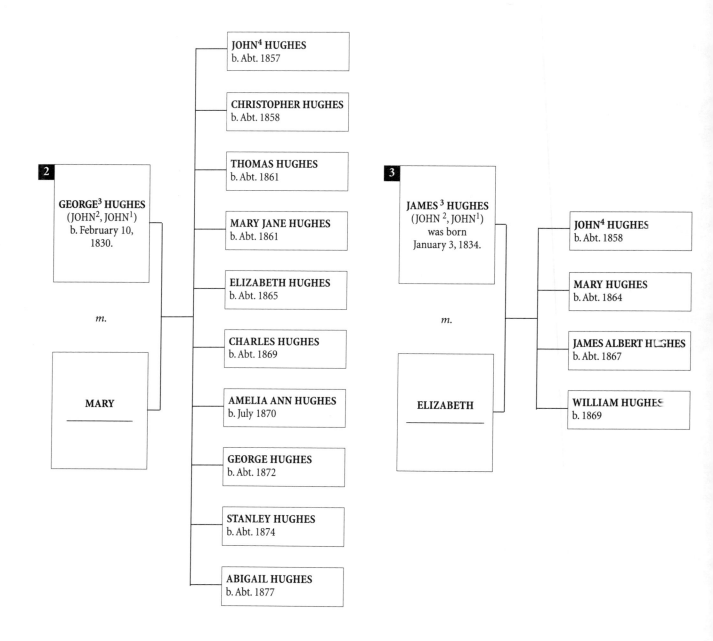

Descendants of John Hughes **Generation No. 2 (#4, #5)**

Descendants of John Hughes **Generation No. 3 (#7)**

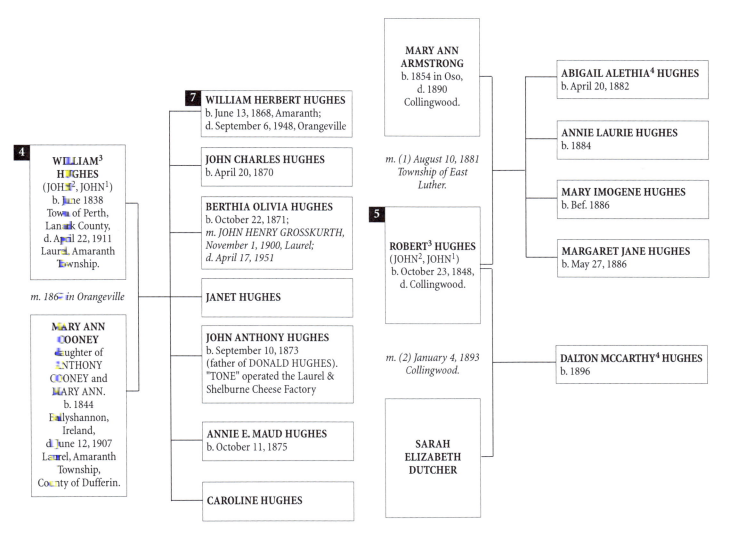

APPENDIX III 237

Descendants of John Hughes **Generation No. 2 (#6)**

Descendants of John Hughes **Generation No. 3 (#8, #9)**

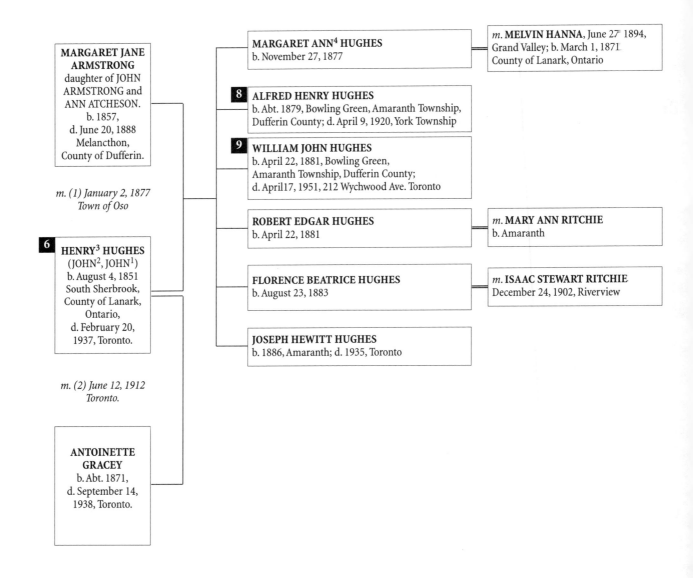

Descendants of John Hughes **Generation No. 3 (#7, #8)**

7

WILLIAM HERBERT[4] HUGHES
(WILLIAM[3], JOHN[2], JOHN[1])
b. June 13, 1868, Amaranth,
d. September 6, 1948 Orangeville.

m. June 21, 1900 in Laurel

JENNIE HENRIETTA GROSSKURTH
b. November 6, 1866,
d. February 20, 1965 Orangeville.

JEAN[5] HUGHES
b. June 15, 1903, Orangeville;
d. August 15, 1956, Orangeville;
Adopted child

8

ALFRED HENRY[4] HUGHES
(HENRY[3], JOHN[2], JOHN[1])
b. Abt. 1879, Bowling Green, Amaranth Township, Dufferin County, d. April 9, 1920, York Township

m. June 15, 1904 in Beeton

PHOEBE MCADAM

CECIL ALFRED[5] HUGHES
b. September 1906

APPENDIX III 239

Descendants of John Hughes
Generation No. 3 (#9)

Descendants of John Hughes
Generation No. 4 (#11, #12, #13)

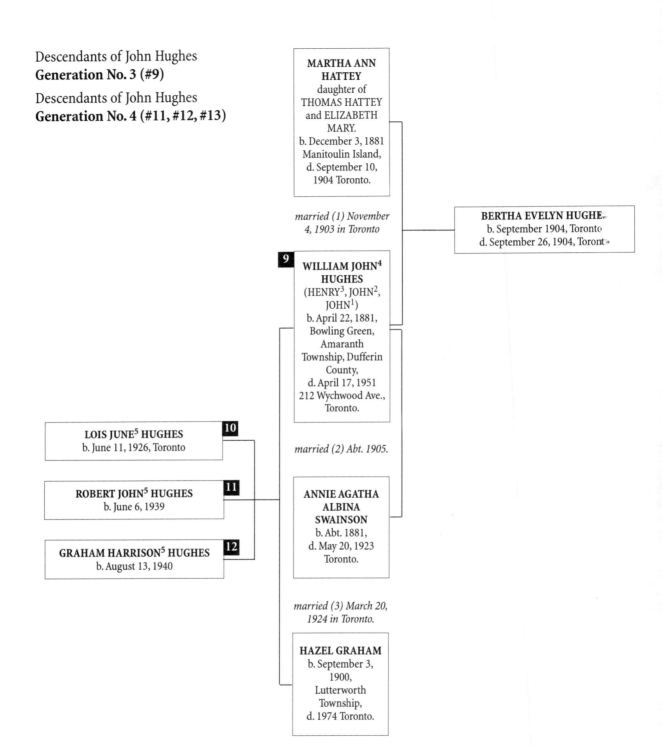

Descendants of John Hughes **Generation No. 4** (#10, #11)

Descendants of John Hughes **Generation No. 5**

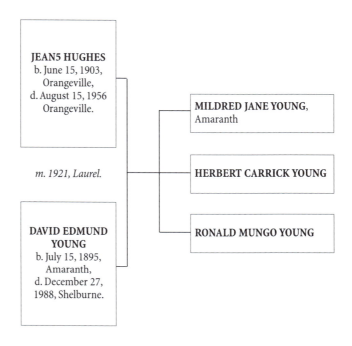

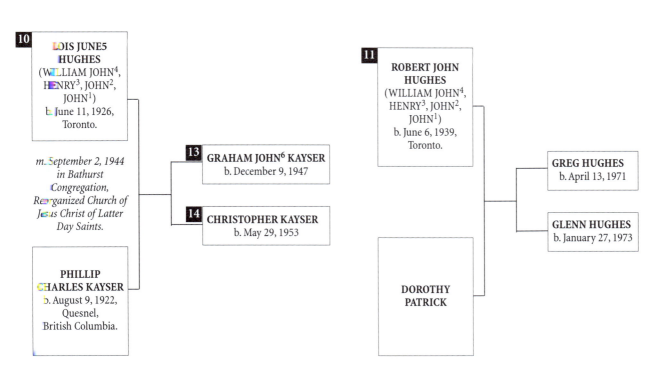

Descendants of John Hughes **Generation No. 4 (#12)**
Descendants of John Hughes **Generation No. 5 (#14)**
Descendants of John Hughes **Generation No. 6 (#15)**
Descendants of John Hughes **Generation No. 7 (#16)**

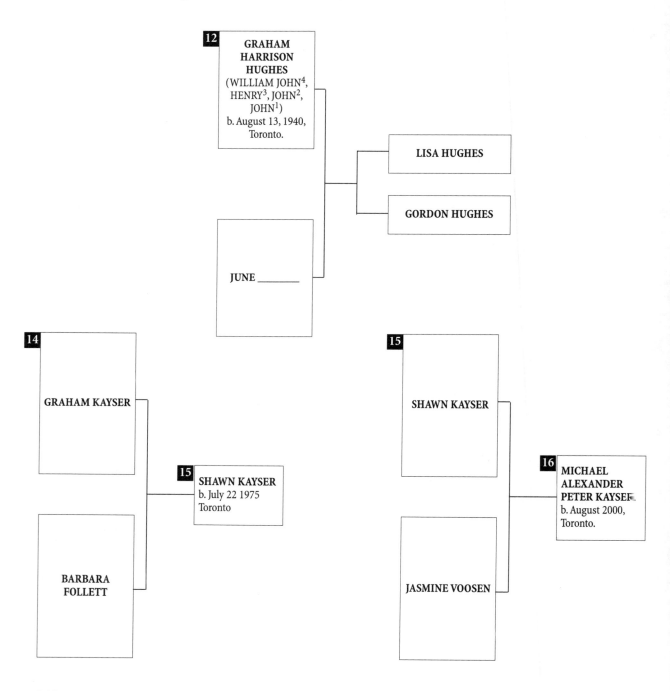

NOTES

PART I

1. Census of Canada 1941, (Review 1871-1941, 8th Census). The population in Dufferin County in 1871 was 16,689; by 1881 it had increased to 22,084.

2. All pupils attending school in Dufferin County learn that the county was named after Lord Dufferin, Frederick Temple Blackwood, who was Governor General in Canada from 1874 to 1878

3. Elizabeth Kelling, *The Roots of Armanth*, (Amaranth Township, 1981) 37.

4. Amaranth Council Minutes, 1854-1900.

5. Elijah Hamilton was the son of Margaret Hughes and John Hamilton and thus a cousin to Jack Hughes.

6. Krista A. Taylor, *Faith of My Forefathers: The Reorganized Church of Jesus Christ of Latter Day saints in East Garafraxa Township, Dufferin County,* unpublished, 1999.

7. A statement of faith that demonstrates beliefs of the Reorganized Church of Jesus Christ of Latter Day Saints: "... We believe that man of God by 'prophecy, and by laying on of hands'... We believe all that God has revealed, all that he does now reveal, and we believe that he will yet reveal many great and important things pertaining to the kingdom of God. We believe in the literal gathering of Israel...that Zion will be built upon this continent, that Christ will reign personally upon the earth...We claim privilege of worshipping Almighty God according to the dictates of our conscience, and allow all men the same privilege,

let them worship how, where, or what they may." Taken from Joseph Smith, "Epitome of Faith" from *Times & Seasons*, Vol. 3, 1842, 710.

8. At the time, it was common practice, should a person lose their farm back to mortgagors, that they would stay on and pay rent until they were in a financial position to buy it again.

9. The Aaronic Priesthood included those men called to the office of "teacher." Their diverse duties consisted, largely of responding to the needs of people through counselling, supporting church attendance and possibly some preaching. "His duties made him a preacher, a class teacher also a visiting officer and a counselor to members" ad defined by the *Church Members Manual*, (Independence, Missouri: Herald Publishing House, 1961) 96.

Part II

1. Glass of the period was packed and shipped in wooden barrels. A minimum order of glass was one barrel as anything less would cause packing problems.

2. "Gray cutting" is a light cut in thin glass, produced by hand-moving a piece of glass against a cutting wheel.

3. After 26 years of production, the "Royal" line was dropped around 1940, as it had been carried by only one or two Toronto stores, one of which was W.R. Kent Jewellery, located on Yonge Street. The only identified examples of the Royal pattern are in the Dufferin County Museum & Archives collection. The 18-piece set of glassware was a gift to Frances and Salisbury Simpson on their 25th wedding anniversary in December, 1917. The set was purchased at W.R. Kent where their daughter Louise Simpson was later employed for over 20 years. Donated by Steve Brown, East Garafraxa, 1999.

4. The Heisey Glass Company of Newark, Ohio was owned by Augustus H. Heisey. The dish is of a shape and size often referred to in glass catalogues of the period as a "Lemon Dish."

5. Interview with Walter McKillop by Karen Carruthers (DCMA staff) in June 2000 at the Dufferin County Museum & Archives.

6. Interview with Lois (Hughes) Kayser by Wayne Townsend, June 2000, in Bobcaygeon, Ontario.

7. Note to Collectors: 'Bobby' Sherriff later ran his own cutting shop in Toronto, employing several cutters. Some of his designs and products bear a label with his name.

8. Identified "depression" glass blanks used by CORN FLOWER from 1927 to 1937 were purchased from Duncan & Miller, Pittsburgh, Pennsylvania; Fostoria Glass Co., Fostoria, Ohio; Heisey Glass, Newark, Ohio; The Imperial Glass Co., Bellaire, Ohio; Lancaster Glass Co., Lancaster, Ohio; New Martinsville Glass Co., New Martinsville, Ohio and Tiffin Glass Co, Tiffin, Ohio.

9. A "turn lot" is the quantity of an item produced from one mold, by one 'glass shop' in a half-day shift, in this period probably from 100 to 150 pieces. Later the quantity increased considerably as technology improved.

10. Little information surrounding the wedding of Hazel Graham and Jack Hughes, not even a photograph, has survived.

11. Interview with J. Sheldon Anderson at Mono in June 1999 by Christine McNeil, Dufferin County Museum & Archives volunteer.

12. Interview with Pete Kayser by Wayne Townsend, June 2000, in Bobcaygeon, Ontario.

13. Interview with Lois (Hughes) Kayser by Wayne Townsend, June 2000, in Bobcaygeon, Ontario.

14. Stanley Knowles, *The New Party*. (Toronto: McClelland & Stewart Limited 1961) 21.

15. Interview with Lois (Hughes) Kayser.

16. From 1939 to 1951 some of the various charities supported by W.J. Hughes were: The Reorganized Church of Jesus Christ Latter Day Saints, Society for Crippled Civilians, Dominion Corps of Legionnaires, Society for Crippled Children, YMCA, Kresge's Toys for Christmas Kids, Forest Hill Police Association, Woodsworth Memorial House Fund, Danforth Lions Circus Funds, Juvenile Football Association, Toronto East General Nurses Alumni Association, and the CNR Veterans Association - Toronto Branch. This information was taken from returned cancelled cheques located in the Dufferin County Museum & Archives Collection.

17. From interview with Pete Kayser.

18. Information taken from *Imperial Glass Encyclopedia*. Vol. I. Marietta, Ohio: National Imperial Glass Collector's Society 1995) 98.

19. Interview with Pete Kayser.

20. The invoice from Ludwik Glass Company in Weston, West Virginia was invoice No. 1572, Order No. 1320 and Order Date October 24, 1943. The invoice and shipping date was July, 1947.

21. Identified blanks used from 1940 to 1950 were purchased from: Duncan and Miller Glass Company of Pittsburgh, Pennsylvania; Federal Glass Company of Columbus, Ohio; Fostoria Glass Company of Fostoria, Ohio; A.H. Heisey Glass Company of Newark, Ohio; Imperial Glass Corporation of Bellaire, Ohio; Indiana Glass Company of Dunkirk, Indiana; Louie Glass Company of Weston, West Virginia; Ludwick Glass Company of Weston, West Virginia; Mid-Atlantic Glass Company of Ellenboro, West Virginia; New Martinsville Glass Company of New Martinsville, Ohio (renamed Viking Glass Company in 1944 or 45); Paden City Glass Company of Paden City, West Virginia and West Virginia Glass Specialties Glass Company of Western, West Virginia. This information was extracted from cancelled cheques and bank statements housed in the Dufferin County Museum & Archives.

22. This was a school established by the Federal Government specifically for veterans of WWII, usually known as a rehabilitation school or rehabilitation program. Here, returning soldiers could upgrade their academic standing or learn new skills, enabling them to integrate back into society.

23. Farquhar (F. J.) McRae was Jack Hughes' lawyer. When he became a provincial judge he left the "Corn Flower" Company.

24. The obituary of W.J. Hughes is taken from the *Dundalk Herald*, April 26, 1951, p.4.

25. Ibid, 2.

26. From ad copy in *The Trader and Canadian Jeweller*. June 1951, page unknown.

Part III

1. Now with W.J. Hughes gone, Hazel Hughes became President; Lois Kayser, Vice President; Pete Kayser, Secretary-Treasurer and Managing Director; F.J. McRae, Director; and auditor Charles E. Baker, Director.

2. Many of these suburban housewives were actually quite isolated from family and former friends and activities. Consequently, they tended to form neighbourly social groups, which frequently included the latest in gossip and household trends. This, in turn, had a positive effect on the sale of CORN FLOWER and other household items.

3. From interviews with Pete and Lois Kayser.

4. In the year 2000, these catalogues in good repair were selling for about $75 each.

5. Interview with Peter Kayser.

6. From the scrapbooks developed by Bob Prouse, now in the Dufferin County Museum & Archives Collection.

7. From the scrapbooks of Bob Prouse.

8. His scrapbooks are organized as to the types of advertising that had been produced while he was with CORN FLOWER: these organizers were Participation Advertising at point of Sale, National Advertising, *Gift Buyer Magazine* Advertising and Co-operative Advertising with retail accounts.

9. From the scrapbooks of Bob Prouse.

10. "Epic," however had demonstrated to the retailers that an old-fashioned, well-known design could be put in a much more modern context and continue to be a best-seller.

11. Shipments of CORN FLOWER were made to: Wright Air Force Base in Dayton, Ohio; R.C.A.F. Joint Staff in Washington, D.C.; Hill Air Force Base in Utah; C.F. (NORAD) Support Unit, Ent Air Force Base, Colorado; Tinker Air Force Base, Oklahoma; McClellan Air Force Base, California; Temple Hills, Maryland; Custer Air Force Base, Michigan and Tullahoma, Tennessee.

12. Interview with Peter Kayser.

13. Taken from the scrapbooks of Bob Prouse, source unknown.//
14. Interview with Peter Kayser.
15. Rod Hanby, "Unique in Glassware" in *Gift Buyer Magazine*, May 1966.
16. Taken from the original legal agreement, donated by Pete and Lois Kayser to the Dufferin County Museum & Archives Collection.
17. Pete Kayser and Bob Prouse serviced the Eaton's stores in Sarnia, three stores in London, Kitchener, Waterloo, Guelph, two stores in Hamilton, St. Catharines and Burlington. In Toronto they serviced the Eaton's stores in The Eaton Centre (formerly Queen St.), College St., Yorkdale Plaza, Sherway Gardens, Scarborough Town Centre, Don Mills Centre, Markville Plaza, Gerrard Shopping Mall and Yonge and Eglinton Mall. In the area surrounding Toronto they serviced Eaton's stores in Brampton, Pickering and Oshawa.
18. The lines chosen were "Croyden," "Janessa," "Nelina," Northwood," Pemberton," Sabrina" and "Venora."
19. Taken from the scrapbooks of Bob Prouse, source unknown.
20. Letter, January 2001, from Chris Kayser, "Some thoughts on my Dad," in the Dufferin County Museum & Archives Collection.
21. Letter from Lucile Kennedy to Wayne Townsend on October 26, 2000. The letter is now in the Dufferin County Museum & Archives Collection.

APPENDIX 1 - CORN FLOWER BLANKS: 1914 TO 1944

1. "Serve It in Coloured Glassware," *Better Homes and Gardens*. September 1929.
2. From an advertisement for CORN FLOWER in *China, Glass and Lamps*, February 12, 1923.
3. Excerpt from advertisement in *Pottery, Glass and Brass Salesman*, December 20, 1934.
4. James Measell, *New Martinsville Glass: 1900-1944*. (Marietta, OH: Antiques Publications, 1994) 166.
5. Ibid, 64.

NOTES FROM CORN FLOWER PLATES

1. Part of a 54-piece set cut by W.J. Hughes as a wedding present to his third wife's friend, Janet Carr, in the 1930s.

2. From the home of Isabella and James Donkin, Riverview. The Donkins were neighbours to the Hughes family in Dufferin County. These pieces have been donated to the Dufferin County Museum & Archives by Isabella Marshall.

3. From the home of Jack and Hazel Hughes, at 212 Wychwood Avenue, Toronto.

4. This Heisey blank was cut by W.J. Hughes for his wife Hazel and used in their home. Donated to the Dufferin County Museum & Archives by Lois (Hughes) and Pete Kayser.

5. This tray was a gift to the Dufferin County Museum & Archives in 2000, from the Canadian Depression Glass Association.

6. Items were cut in the late 1930s by CORN FLOWER cutter Mike Gray of Melancthon township for his future wife, Theresa. Donated to the Dufferin County Museum & Archives by Theresa Gray.

7. Part of a 24-piece set, found in Montreal in 2000 by Wayne Townsend. The set was purchased for the Dufferin County Museum & Archives.

8. From the home of W.J. and Hazel Hughes at 212 Wychwood Avenue, Toronto.

9. Donated to the Dufferin County Museum & Archives in 1999 from the home of Lois (Hughes) and Pete Kayser.

SELECTED BIBLIOGRAPHY

Bickenheuser, Frid, *Tiffin Glassmasters II.* Grove City, Ohio: Glassmasters Publication, 1981.

Bredehoft, Neila and Tom, *The Collector's Encyclopedia of Heisey Glass, 1925-1938.* Paducah, Kentucky: Collector Books, 1993.

Goshe, Ed; Hemminger, Ruth and Pina, Leslie, *Depression Era Stems & Tableware Tiffin.* Atglen, Pennsylvania: Schiffer Publishing, 1998.

Long, Milbra and Seate, Emily, *Fostoria Tableware, 1924-1943.* Paducah, Kentucky: Collector Books: 1999.

Measell, James and Wiggins, Berry, *Great American Glass of the Roaring 20s & Depression Era.* Marietta, Ohio: Antique Publications, 1998.

Measell, James, *New Martinsville Glass, 1900-1944.* Marietta, Ohio: Antique Publications, 1994.

Measell, James, ed. *Imperial Glass Encyclopedia, Vol. I.* National Imperial Glass Collector's Society. Marietta, Ohio: The Glass Press Inc., 1995.

Pina, Leslie and Gallagher, Jerry, *Tiffin Glass, 1914-1940.* Atglen, Pennsylvania: Schiffer Publishing, 1996.

Vogel, Clarence W., *Heisey's Art and Colored Glass, 1922-1942.* Plymouth, Ohio: Heisey Publications, 1970.

Weatherman, Hazel Marie, *Coloured Glassware of the Depression Era 2.* Springfield, Missouri: Weatherman Glassbooks, 1974.

CREDITS FOR VISUALS

All visuals used are the property of the Dufferin County Museum & Archives Collection and are used with permission.

a. All colour photographs, the b&w visual of the cutting frame and the photograph of the author are the work of Peter Herlihy of Orangeville.

b. The b&w photographs from the 1930s "photograph/catalogue" were done by J. Thornley Wrench of Toronto, as commissioned by W.J. Hughes "Corn Flower."

c. The b&w photographs from the 1953 CORN FLOWER catalogue are the work of Panda Photographers of Toronto, as contracted by W.J. Hughes and Sons "Corn Flower" Limited.

d. All family photographs and CORN FLOWER memorabilia were donated to the Dufferin County Museum & Archives by Lois (Hughes) and Pete Kayser.

e. Family Tree research by Krista Taylor of East Garafraxa.

f. Maps by Darrell Keenie of Dufferin County Museum & Archives.

g. Sketch of CORNFLOWER design by Linda McLaren of Amaranth.

INDEX

A
A.H. Heisey Glass Company (see Heisey Glass Co.)
A.J. Beatty and Sons, 230
Acorn Anodizing Co. Ltd., 171
Allen's Stationery, 144
Alliston (ON), 47
American Flint, 226, 248
Anderson, J. Sheldon (Shelly), 56, 245
Andrew, Sue (Jones) (Mrs. Arthur), 152
Anglican, 16
Armstrong:
   Ann (Atcheson) (Mrs. John), 22
   John Y., 22
   Margaret Jane (see Margaret Jane Hughes)
Atcheson, Ann (see Ann Armstrong)
Atlantic City Glass and China Show, 199, 203

B
B. P. Service Stations, 176
Baker, Charles E., 138, 247
Ball, Tom, 93, 122
Barrie (ON), 47
Bayes, Bill, 90
Beading, 43, 49, 50
Beeton (ON), 33
Belfast (Ireland), 21
Beligum, 152, 181
Bellaire (OH)., 122, 145
Better Homes and Gardens, 216, 246
Berry Pink Industries, 202
Birks Jewellery, 12
Blackwood, Frederic Temple (Marquis of Dufferin and Ava), 19, 243
Booth, __ Mr., 95
Book of Mormon, 24
Bowlerama, 175
Bowling Green (settlement), 15, 16, 19, 24, 214
Brampton (ON), 18, 19, 45
Breathet, Jack, 90
Brigdens Printers, 125
Brown, John, 20
Brown, Steve, 212, 244
Buchanans (the), 21
Budapest, 180, 188

C
CCF (see Co-operative Commonwealth Federation)
Caledon (ON), 54
Calgary (AB), 36
Cambridge Glass Factory, 231
Camp Borden, 86
Canadian Armed Services, 164
Canadian Bride, 149
Canadian Depression Glass Association, 214, 249
Canadian Jeweller, 201
Canadian Jewellers Association, 40, 52
Canadian National Exhibition (CNE), 158, 160, 162
Canadian Pacific Railway, 18
Candlewick (see Imperial Glass Company)
Caramia (see Ferunion)
Cariad (see Ferunion)
Carnival glass, 165
Carruthers, Karen, 244
Cathcart, Robert, 20
Carr, Jeanette, 54, 116, 249
Chatelaine, 150, 151, 183
China, Glass and Lamps, 246
Church of England, 21
Cleave, Beth, 214
Collingwood (ON), 47
Columbus (OH), 192, 206
Concord (ON), 208
Cooney, Anthony, 21
Cooney, Mary Ann (see Mary Ann Hughes), 21
Co-operative Commonwealth Federation (CCF), 76, 77
Cosmos (see R.G. Sheriff)
Corbetton Methodist Church Building, 213
Corn Flower:
   Foil label(s), 63, 83, 124, 183, 193
   Moderne stemware, 162
   Number 73, 61, 63, 70, 84, 142, 180
   Number 85, 61, 62, 84, 142, 181
   Number 196, 61, 62, 70, 84, 142, 146, 180, 181, 189
   Number 200, 142
   Number 281 (see Imperial Glass)
   Ovenware, 192, 193
   Premium, 177
   Snow Flower (Belgium), 15, 124, 152, 159, 160
   Tumblers, 194
Corinna stemware (Czechoslovakia), 142
Corn Flower Festival, 212-21_
Cowansville (PQ), 85
Credit Valley Railway, 18
Crescent Window Glasswork, 231
Crow's Foot design (manufacturer unknown), 111
Crozier, Hugh (Rev.), 30
Crystal glass, 216
County of Armagh (Ireland), 2_
Country Store Products, 202-204
Curtis, Bill, 82, 90, 139
Cutler Brands Ltd., 164, 179, 192, 194
cutting frame(s), 88, 89, 139, 140, 141
Czechoslovakia, 83-85, 142, 180

D
D.C. Taylor & Son, 144
Depression (Years), 68, 76, 77, 78, 118, 218
Depression Glass, 216-218, 245
Dixon, Joseph, 20
Dominion Census, 15, 16, 22, 243
Donkin, Isabella, 249
Donkin, James, 249
Dufferin County, 11, 13, 17-20, 22, 30, 37, 46, 54, 60, 65, 70, 78, 83, 85, 94, 210, 214, 215, 243, 249

Dufferin County Museum & Archives (DCMA), 13, 14,, 34, 70, 80, 83, 127, 140, 149, 160, 185, 209-213, 215, 225, 227, 235, 244, 245, 248, 249
Duncan and Miller Glass Company, 245, 246
Dundalk Herald, 94, 246
Dynes, Robert, 85

E

Eaton's (Department Store), 47, 48, 51, 142, 143, 159, 160, 169, 174, 176, 180, 199, 200, 209
Eilers Jewellers, 144
Elegant Glassware (hand glass), 217-220, 222, 223, 225, 228, 231
Ellenboro (WV), 207
Ellis-Fyrie Ltd., 12
End of Day Ruby glassware, 165
English Settlement (Laurel), 20
Epic glassware (see Viking Class)

F

Federal Box Company, 206
Federal Glass Company, 192, 206, 246
Fenton Art Glass Company, 167, 169, 190, 206
Fenton Milk Glass, 169, 191, 202-204, 206
Fenton, Frank, 206
Fenton, Wilbur "Bill," 167, 206
Ferunion Glass, 179, 180, 181, 185, 187, 201, 206
   Caramia, 195, 202
   Cariad, 202
   Janessa, 206
   Venora, 206
Fischer Glass Company, 167
Fisher, David, 228
Fostoria Glass Company, 218, 220, 225, 231, 245, 246
   Fostoria pieces, 219
Fox, Harold G. (Dr.) Q.C., 234
French Cannon Ball pattern, 223
Fringing (see also nicking), 50, 51
Frontenac County, 16, 22

G

Gamble, Ken, 13
Gardner, A.B., 183

George Watts Jewellery (Shelburne), 65
Gerrity Metal Products, 204
Gestetner Company, 197
Gibson, Gloria (see Gloria Myers)
Gift Buyer, 156-159, 187, 190, 247, 248
Glass Export of Prague, 85
Grace Memorial Hospital (Toronto), 53, 116
Grace Hospital School of Nursing, 53
Gracey, Antoinette (see Antoinette Hughes)
Graham, Annie (see Annie McAdam)
Graham, Hazel (see Hazel Hughes)
Grand Valley (ON), 30, 214
Gray:
   Georgina (see Georgina Peace)
   Matthew Stickney (Rev.), 20
   William Morris "Mike," 70, 80, 82, 90, 139, 214, 249
   Theresa (Mrs. W.M.), 70, 80, 249
Gray (cut) cutting, 40, 43, 45, 244
Grey County, 18, 24
Grogan, Jimmy, 54
Guelph (ON), 47

H

Haddy, Body and Company (Toronto), 70, 218
Haliburton area, 53
Hamburgh (Germany), 84
Hamilton:
   Elijah, 22, 243
   John, 21, 243
   John (missionary), 24
   Margaret (Hughes) (Mrs. John), 21, 243
   Samuel, 22
Hammond, Turner & Sons Limited (UK), 61
Handby, Rod, 190, 248
Hanna, Margaret Ann "Annie" (Hughes), 16, 22, 30, 32, 36, 238
Hanna, Melvin, 30, 32, 36, 238
Hartland (NB), 85
Hartley Jewellery, 195

Hattey:
   Elizabeth Mary, 32
   Martha Ann (see Martha Ann Hughes)
   Thomas, 32
Hayes, Margaret (see Margaret Swainson)
Heisey, Augustus H., 220, 244
Heisey Glass Company, 43, 218, 220-222, 225, 231, 244, 246, 249
   Empress line #1401, 220
   Fern line #1495, 220, 221
   Mars #113, 222
   Heisey selected items (attributed), 73, 75
Henry Glover and Co., 138
Hinton, Thomas, 16
Hocking Glass Company, 225
Hogarth's of Napanee, 65
Holiday Silverplate, 202, 203
Houston, __ (Mr.), 142
Houston, Jack, 142
Hughes (family): 25, 26, 34
   Abigail (White) (Mrs. John Sr.), 21, 235
   Alfred Henry, 16, 22, 23, 32, 36, 60, 238, 239
   Annie Agatha Albina (Swainson), 33-36, 48, 93, 240
   Antoinette (Gracey) (2nd Mrs. Henry), 36, 59, 235, 238
   Bertha Evelyn, 32, 240
   Cecil, Alfred, 60, 239
   Donald "Don", 14, 59, 213, 237
   Elizabeth (__) (Mrs, James), 235, 236
   Elizabeth (__) (Mrs. Joseph), 22
   Florence Beatrice (Flossie) (see Florence Ritchie)
   George, 235, 236
   Glenn, 241
   Graham Harrison, 78, 89, 93, 94, 240, 242
   Greg, 241
   Harold, 60
   Hazel, 60
   Hazel (Graham) (3rd Mrs. W.J.), 53-56, 59, 60, 66, 78, 86, 88, 89, 92, 94, 95, 114-117, 138, 214, 240, 245, 247, 249
   Henrietta "Jennie" (__) (Mrs. Herbert), 66

Henry, 16, 17, 19, 21-24, 26, 27, 36, 59, 94, 235, 238
Herbert, 66
Isabella (__) (Mrs. John), 22
James, 235, 236
Jean (see Jean Young)
Jennie Henrietta (Grosskurth) (Mrs. Wm Herbert), 237
John (cousin), 22
John (grandfather), 21, 22, 235
John Anthony (Tone), 21, 59, 237
Joseph, 22, 26, 235
Joseph Hewitt, 22, 36, 37, 60, 238
Lloyd, 60, 82, 90, 138, 139
Lois June (see Lois Kayser)
Maisie, 60
Margaret (see Margaret Hamilton)
Margaret Ann (Annie), (see Margaret Ann Hanna)
Margaret Jane (Armstrong) (1st Mrs. Henry), 16, 17, 19, 22, 23, 26, 94, 235, 238
Martha Ann (Hattey) (1st Mrs. W.J.), 32, 33, 240
Mary (__) (Mrs. George), 235, 236
Mary Ann (Armstrong) (Mrs. Robert), 235, 237
Mary Ann (Cooney) (Mrs. William), 20, 235
Mary Ann "Minnie" (Ritchie) (Mrs. Robert E.), 36, 60, 238
Maude (Dobbin) (Mrs. John Anthony), 20, 59
Phoebe (McAdam) (Mrs. Alfred), 33, 36, 60, 239
Robert (uncle), 81, 235, 237
Robert Edgar "Bob," 16, 19, 22, 23, 30, 31, 36, 56, 59, 60, 82, 88, 238
Robert John, 78, 89, 93, 94, 240, 241
Sarah Elizabeth (Dutcher) (2nd Mrs. Robert), 235, 237
William, 20, 21, 235. 237
William Herbert (Herb), 21, 25, 237, 238
William John (W.J.) "Jack," 11-13, 16, 19, 20, 22, 26-61, 65-72, 76-81, 83-86, 88-96, 113-116, 121, 142, 165, 178, 203, 209-211, 213, 214, 216-222, 228, 232,

234, 238, 240, 245-247, 249
Hughes No. 412 crystal Candy Box, 73
Hudson's Bay Company, 143
Hungary, 180, 187, 189, 195, 201, 202, 207
Hungarian Trading Company for Technical Goods (Ferunion), 180

I
Imperial Glass Corporation, 80, 93, 120-122, 127, 128, 145, 152, 159, 165, 167, 185, 190, 204, 207, 209, 218, 221-224, 245, 246
  Imperial Candlewick, 11, 80, 81, 111, 120, 121, 127-132, 149, 152, 154, 161, 164, 191, 204, 205, 209, 210, 213, 222, 223
  Imperial Carnival Glass, 202
  Imperial Number '281', 122-124, 127, 129
  Imperial Pie Crust Crystal, 81
  Imperial Vintage Milk Glass, 149, 154, 165
Indiana Glass Company, 206, 246
Ireland, 19, 21
Irving Rice Company, 164

J
J. Russell Morrow Jeweller (Orangeville), 56, 65
Japan, 164
Jarvis, Frederick, 26, 27, 33
Johnny Martin's Fina Service Station, 176
Junior Magazine, 165

K
Kayser:
  Christopher Stephen, 114, 148, 208, 241, 242, 248
  Graham John, 90, 93, 196-198, 208, 241
  Lois June (Hughes) (Mrs. P.C.), 14, 40, 54, 55, 65, 66, 68, 76, 79, 86, 87, 89, 92, 94, 114, 115, 138, 145, 148, 149, 187, 188, 196, 203, 209-213, 232, 240, 241, 244. 247-249
  Michael Alexander Peter, 242
  Phillip Charles "Pete," 14, 86-89, 91, 92, 95, 113, 114, 120, 122, 125, 126, 134-138, 142-146, 148, 149, 152-154, 162, 164, 167, 170, 173-175, 177-181, 185, 187-190, 195-197, 199, 200, 203, 206, 208-213, 221, 232, 234, 241, 245-249
  Shawn, 117, 242
Keenie, Darrell, 212
Kelly, Don, 86,
Kennedy, Lucile J., 209, 221, 248
Kenwood Avenue, 88, 90, 94, 113, 114, 133, 134, 140, 142, 197
Kerr's Jewellery, 85
Kleiner, E.C. "Ed," 80, 93, 152, 159
Kolb, Willard, 223

L
Lakefield Preparatory School for Boys, 116
Lambton County, 33
Lanark County, 16, 20-22, 30
Lancaster Glass Co., 100, 104, 105, 109, 110, 218, 223, 225, 245
  Lancaster #88, 224
  Lancaster #879, 223, 224
Lanyon's Jewellery (NB), 85
Laurel (hamlet) (see also English Settlement and Richardson's Corners), 16, 20, 22, 24, 66, 94
Lavery Jewellers, 144
Lead crystal, 39-42, 136, 145, 161, 162, 165, 196, 201, 202
League for Social Reconstruction, 76
Leaside (Toronto), 85
Lemiski, Walter T., 214, 232
Little, __ (Mrs. Lloyd), 95
London (ON), 25, 47
Louie Glass Company, 246
Ludwik Glass Company, 82, 119, 246

M
Maclean's, 150
Macphail, Agnes Campbell, 76
Manitoulin Island, 32
Markle, __ (Mrs. P.), 95
Marshall, Isabella, 249
Martin, Lucien, 225
Martin, Philip, 225
Martin, Rich, 30
McAdam:
  Annie (Graham) (Mrs. Bill), 60
  Bill, 60, 90
  Ernie, 90
  Phoebe (see Phoebe Hughes)
McDougal and Brown Funeral Home, 93, 94
McIntosh, J.A., 24
McKee Glass Company, 223
  Rays, 223
McKillop, Walter, 45, 244
McLeod, Jessie (Graham), 54
McLeod, Murray, 214
McNeil, Christine, 245
McRae, F.J., 92, 143, 246, 247
McWilliams, Paul, 208
Merkley, Bill, 90
Methodist(s), 20, 24, 56, 214
Mid-Atlantic Glass Company, 207, 246
Mono Mills (ON), 54
Montreal Gift Show, 155
Mortimer, A.E., 32
Mount Pleasant Cemetery (Toronto), 32, 33
Mount Pleasant Mausoleum, 48, 93
Murray's Express (Toronto), 85
Myers, Fred, 120, 125, 126, 136, 138, 143, 148, 155, 170, 192
Myers, Gloria (Gibson), 120, 148

N
Napanee (ON), 65
National Gift Show, 154
New Martinsville Glass Company, 73, 74,106-108, 218, 219, 225-228, 245, 246
  Janice-Line #45, 107, 108
  Moondrops-Line #37, 225, 226
  "Our New Candy Box De Luxe" Line #103, 227
  Radiance - Line #42 (Tear Drop), 132, 221, 225, 226
  New Martinsville items, 219
  New Martinsville selected items (attributed), 74
Newton, Earl W., 223
Nicking (fringing), 50-52, 141

O
Oakville (ON), 19
O'Connor Bowl, 176
O'Connor Fast Car Wash, 176
Olympia (lead crystal), 160, 161
Ontario Heritage Act, 18
Orange Lodge, 16
Orangeville (ON), 15, 18, 19, 37, 47, 56, 214
Oshawa (ON), 47
Ostrander:
  Ernie, 85
  Jack, 85
  Ken, 85
  Neil, 85
  Vic, 85
Ottawa (ON), 65
Owen Sound (ON), 16

P
Paden City Glass Manufacturing Company, 218, 227, 246
Palgrave (ON), 54, 79
Palmer Jewellers, 144
Panda Photographers, 125, 127
Pangborne sandblasting cabinet, 147
Parks Jewellers, 144
Peace, "Bud," 82, 90
Peace, Georgina (Gray), 82
Peoples Jewellers Ltd., 209
Peterborough (ON), 116
Phillips Glass Ltd., 12
Photograph/Catalogue (1937), 69
Pittsburg China and Glass Show, 145
Poland, 83
Pottery, Glass and Brass Salesman, 225, 248
Premium line (see Corn Flower)
Presbyterian(s), 20
Protestant(s), 24
Prouse, (A.R.) Robert "Bob," 143, 159, 160, 164, 169, 170, 180, 185, 187-189, 191, 195, 196, 199, 200, 203, 210, 221, 247, 248

Q
Quesnel (BC), 86, 87

R
RCAF (Royal Canadian Air Force), 82, 86, 87
R.T. Holman Limited, 152
Rainbow Art Glass, 202
Redickville (ON), 85
Regina Manifesto, 77
Reid, Thomas F., 15, 16

Reid's Jewellery (BC), 85
Reorganized Church of Jesus
    Christ of Latter Day Saints
    (RLDS), 24, 25, 30, 32, 34, 76,
    86, 94, 95, 243
  Aaronic Priesthood, 34, 244
  Epitome of Faith, 24, 244
  Religio, 34
Richardson's Corners (Laurel),
    20
Riky, Susan, 26
Ritchie:
  Florence (Flossie) Beatrice
    (Hughes), 22, 23, 30, 36, 238
  Isaac Stewart, 30, 36, 238
  Mary Ann "Minnie" (see
    Mary Ann Hughes)
Riverview (village), 22, 24, 26-
    28, 30, 32, 60, 70, 76, 94, 95,
    214, 248, 249
Robinson, Florence (Graham),
    54
Roden, Frank, 39, 45
Roden, Thomas, 39
Roden Brothers (Silversmiths)
    (Silverware and Cut Glass)
    Ltd., 12, 29, 30, 32, 34, 36, 39-
    42, 45, 66, 93
Royal Ice, 40, 44, 244
Royal Canadian Mounted
    Police, 171
Royal Canadian Navy, 116
Ruby-footed beer stein, 83
Ruby-footed pilsner glass, 83

S
Saint's Herald, 95
"Serve It in Coloured
    Glassware," 216, 246
Scace:
  John, 95
  George, 60, 82, 214
  ___ (Mrs. John), 95
  Harry A., 27
Shelburne (ON), 13, 19, 21, 26,
    27, 65, 197
Shelburne Cemetery, 26
Shelburne Free Press &
    Economist, The, 26, 30
Sheriff, R.G. "Bobby," 47, 82, 83,
    84, 245
  Cosmos, 82, 234
Silk, Aubrey "Bobby," 197, 214
Silk, Ellen, 197
Simcoe County, 18

Simpson:
  Frances, 244
  Louise, 244
  Salisbury, 244
Simpsons (Department Store)
    (Robert Simpson), 47, 48,
    143, 164, 176
Slag glass, 165
Smith, Joseph, 24, 242
Snow Flower (see Corn Flower)
Social Gospel Movement, 76
Spence, James, 20
St. Matthew's Anglican Church
    (Laurel), 20
Stanley Manufacturing
    (Toronto), 63
Streetsville (ON), 18
Supreme Aluminum Products,
    170-173, 179
Swainson:
  Annie Agatha Albina (see
    Annie Hughes)
  Earl, 33
  John G., 33
  Margaret (Hayes), 33
Swedish Glass Imports, 142
Szenkouits Limited, 84

T
T.M. Palmer Jewellers, 144
Taylor, Krista, 214, 241
Taylor, Loraine (Mrs.), 138
Taylor, Mildred (Young), 66, 214
Tear Drop (see New
    Martinsville)
Thompson's Jewellery, 85
Tiffin Glass Company, 97-102,
    110, 218, 223, 228-231, 245
  Tiffin #3 cream/sugar, 223
  Tiffin #6 cream/sugar, 223
  Tiffin #14185 cream/sugar, 223
  Tiffin 4" Candleholder #342,
    75
  Tiffin footed Tumblers 315020,
    72, 228
  Tiffin stemware #15024, 228,
    229
Toronto Board of Trade, 94
Toronto Gift Show, 155, 195, 203
Toronto Glass & Mirror Co.
    (Advance Glass), 57
Toronto, Grey & Bruce Railway,
    16, 18
Townsend, Wayne, 14, 212, 244,
    245, 248, 249

Township of Albion (Peel), 54
Township of Amaranth
    (Dufferin), 15, 16, 19-22, 24,
    214
Township of Bathurst (Lanark),
    22
Township of Egremont (Grey),
    24
Township of Luther (Dufferin),
    19
Township of Lutterworth
    (Haliburton), 53
Township of Melancthon
    (Dufferin), 19, 22, 24, 26, 27,
    30, 36, 82
Township of Mono (Dufferin),
    56
Township of Oso (Frontenac),
    22
Township of Proton (Grey), 76
Township of South Sherbrooke
    (Lanark), 21
Township of York (York), 36
*Trader and Canadian Jeweller,
    The*, 95, 138, 246
Tycos Drive (North York), 134,
    137, 165, 167, 197, 208

U
United Glass and Ceramic
    Workers of North America,
    185
United States Glass Company,
    223, 230
  Atlas line, 223
University of Toronto, 86, 146
Upper Canada, 16, 21, 22

V
Viking Glass Company, 162, 163,
    167, 169, 185, 187, 190, 191,
    203, 207, 226, 227, 246
  Epic, 162-164, 202, 247
  Princess, 187
  Ruby Glass, 206
  Visterama, 167-169
Vintage Milk Glass (see
    Imperial Vintage Milk
    Glass)
Visterama (see Viking Glass
    Co.)
Vogel, Clarence W., 221

W
W.J. Hughes and Son, 78

W.J. Hughes and Sons, 78, 80,
    81, 86, 89, 90, 94
W.J. Hughes and Sons "Corn
    Flower" Limited, 16, 77, 80,
    83, 87, 90, 92, 113, 120-122,
    124, 125, 127, 137, 143, 145, 149-
    151, 160-162, 164, 165, 167, 170.
    172, 175, 176, 181, 183, 185, 187,
    188, 190, 191, 192, 194, 197,
    201-203, 205, 208-210, 214,
    218, 220-229, 231, 232
W. R. Kent Jeweller, 244
Waddell, Charles, 69
Walker cutting machines, 145,
    160, 174-176
Walker, Victor, 146
Walsh Advertising Company,
    120, 138, 148, 155, 170, 192, 233
Waterford (ON), 195
Wellington County, 18, 21
West Germany, 160, 161, 165
West Virginia, 82, 217, 218, 228
West Virginia Glass Specialities
    Company, 131, 218, 231, 246
Weston Glass Company, 231
White, Abigail (see Abigail
    Hughes)
White, Bonnie, 214
Whittington (hamlet), 22
Windsor (ON), 65
Wohinc, Louie, 231
World War I, 46, 47, 159, 216
World War II, 70, 80-83, 118, 216,
    229, 246
Wrench, J. Thornley, 69, 72-75,
    218
Wychwood Avenue (Toronto),
    34, 36, 37, 40, 44, 48, 54-58,
    76, 88, 89, 94, 114, 117, 140,
    190, 214, 249

XYZ
York East (constituency), 76
York South (constituency), 76
Young, David Edmund, 241
Young, Jean (Hughes), 66, 239,
    241

ABOUT THE AUTHOR

Wayne Townsend was born in Dufferin County in East Luther township. A lifelong collector, Wayne purchased his first antique, a Benningtonware bowl, at age 12. Wayne has been involved in several restorations of historic buildings in Orangeville including the Opera House and Market and the Dufferin County Courthouse, as well as actively participating in numerous community historic organizations. After an 18-year career in Graphic Art, Wayne Townsend became the curator of the Dufferin County Museum and Archives in 1988 and opened their new facility in 1994. Since then, he has focused on building the collection of artifact and archival material for the facility. In the last two years, since discovering the Dufferin County connection to W.J. Hughes "Corn Flower," the museum has collected over 500 pieces of Corn Flower and catalogued the archival materials of the company. Wayne is an advocate of local Canadian heroes being celebrated in their communities.